Leilah Publications

Ipsissimus

To order wholesale, and bulk please contact:
American Wholesale Book Company (205) 956-4151
Ingram Book Company (800) 937-8000
Baker & Taylor (800) 775-1100

Leilah Publications P.O. Box 1863 Tempe, AZ 85280 U.S.A.
http://leilah.org

Leilah Publications is an underground publishing company producing & investing in cutting edge, avante-garde artists, writers, musicians, and entertainers. Our artistic material explores the boundaries of human consciousness, psychology, and sexuality by using literature, poetry, music, art, the occult, and theatre. Leilah Publications is a publishing company for the 21st century, not the 20th.

IPSISSIMUS

E.A. KOETTING

Table of Contents

Foreword

Pushing the boundaries of what was considered acceptable and sane even in the insane world of the occult, author, adventurer, metaphysician, mystic, yogi, and ritual magician Aleister Crowley became pariah not only to political and religious factions but also to his own brotherhood of occult practitioners, being ousted from the very groups that he had helped bring to power, namely the Hermetic Order of the Golden Dawn, the vivification of which he was a central figure.

In the early 1900s, Crowley formed new groups and lodges wherein he could continue not only to teach that which he had learned in his occult career, but also to continue in his own process of Ascent. One such order, the Ordo Astrum Argentum, the Order of the Silver Star, bore his deepest and most ascendant teachings with the greatest clarity.

While the Hermetic Order of the Golden Dawn would take on the task of teaching the secrets of the esoteric arts to its adherents, the A.:.A.:. assumed that those in its ranks would already possess the knowledge and faculties necessary for the higher spiritual operations.

The Ordo Astrum Argentum, in contrast to the Hermetic Order of the Golden Dawn and Crowley's own fraternal society of the Ordo Templi Orientis, held very few group rituals, the guidelines and instructions for the various initiations passed from mentor to apprentice alone. In a period when all that was once clandestine was being risen to eye-level, the A.:.A.:. remained a true secret society.

The Order, which Crowley only referred to as "A.:.A.:.," held eleven degrees of initiation, progressing from a Probationer, to the highest degree of spiritual attainment: Ipsissimus.

In his legendary work, Magick in Theory and Practice, Crowley writes, regarding this highest rank:

"Ipsissimus. --- Is beyond all this and beyond all comprehension.

"Here it is only said this: The Ipsissimus is wholly free from all limitations soever, existing in the nature of all things without discriminations of quantity or quality between them. He has identified Being and not-Being and Becoming, action and non-action and tendency to action, with all other such triplicities, not distinguishing between them in respect of any conditions, or between any one thing and any other thing as to whether it is with or without conditions.

"The Ipsissimus has no relation as such with any Being: He has no will in any direction, and no Consciousness of any kind involving duality, for in Him all is accomplished."[1]

The whole of Crowley's work and teachings, from the opening of the Aethyrs to the Knowledge and Conversation of the Holy Guardian Angel, had the single aim of the attainment of this state, of embodying Ipsissimus. Indeed, this is the unspoken and unwritten aim of every spiritual path.

While neither this book nor this author adheres in the slightest measures to the teachings of Aleister Crowley or the A.·.A.·., no term could quite summarize the final goal of Ascent as succinctly as Ipsissimus.

And again from Crowley's comments on this, the most mysterious grade of the A.·.A.·., from <u>Magick in Theory and Practice</u>, "He is sworn to accept this Grade in the presence of a witness, and to express its nature in word and deed, but to withdraw Himself at once within the veils of his natural manifestation as a man, and to keep silence during his human life as to the fact of his attainment, even to the other members of the Order."

Introduction

    My father didn't help me build my wings. In fact, he considered that the entire feat and even my consideration of it was a waste of time. I should instead be focused on economics, academics, on finding something stable, something earthy onto which my mind should be fixed. My mother considered the task of rising higher through such a flight than even Babel could offer to be a demonic task, an inception not of my own genius, but of the minds of conspiring cultists who had obviously led me astray.

    But the Sun was there, beyond the sky. Not the solar orb that gives light to the flora and the fauna and the critters crawling the crevices of the crusted earth, but a sun that only I seemed to see, a center of Light and Glory, whose rays condensed as energy and matter and thought and feeling, into all of the worlds below. It was to this Sun, this Eternal Source, that I intended to fly.

Simply fastening waxen wings with harnesses around my torso would not accomplish the outrageous task at hand. No, I would have to construct a mechanism which would endure heat and wind and rain and the obvious pressure of the flight itself.

My body, the very same and original organism of my physical construction, would become my wings. I strengthened this organism through a dialectic discipline, starving it to ensure that it would prevail through hunger, letting it sit in the cold through the nights unprotected as to ensure its durability through hardship, exposing it to desert heats without clothing to condition it to withstand such solar devastation, and then working it under heavy loads so that it would not crumble at the critical moment of the flight.

The day arrived for me to fly, to soar towards that sun. It was not a day that I had pre-determined. I had not marked it on a calendar. I had not scheduled it in my planner. But the sun called to me on that day, and told me to come, whispering that all of the doorways and windows were opened. And so I harnessed my body onto myself, as my wings, and I stood on the rocky earth beneath me, the granulates of desert sand itching between my toes, and I began to lift, slowly at first, but once the motion had begun, there was nothing I could do to slow it.

Wind whipped through the feathers on my back and stung my eyes as the invisible current pulled tears across my face. The buildings that were once so high above me passed below like a simple model of a thing to be constructed, the cars and boats and even the airplanes beneath me being recognized in their sheer primitiveness, as I, unaided by any other mechanism than my body, soared above it all, towards the sun, becoming blinded by its glory, sweat streaking down my reddening skin.

Rather than burning me, however, the sun accepted me into its grace as I neared it, all of the planets and the lights and the stars fading into meaninglessness as the first tier of glory was reached, the phantoms of the spirit dancing across my spotted vision. Just as the ancient gods embraced me, I sank deeper into the sun, into the middle of it, into the second tier, my ears humming with the knowledge of all things, time being eradicated from my understanding, all events and ideas at all times converging in a choir of silence. And as the bodhisattvas whispered to me, a door opened to the core of the sun, to the very center of the whole thing. Image disappeared. Form disappeared. Thought disappeared. I was no longer a visitor to the sun, but I was the sun, the rays of my light streaming into the blackness of space, lighting up the spheres circled around me. For a moment, I was God.

As the rapture of that realization took me, and as I smiled at the wonder of it, the bodhisattvas greeted me again, and then the phantoms, and then the sun drifted farther away. I wasn't sure what was happening until I was already in the earth's relentless pull, my body soaring a million times faster than I had flown, not towards the sun, not towards my beautiful absolution, but towards the dust, feathers whistling as the wind ripped them from my wings.

My bloodied and burnt body slammed to the ground, but I stood, near featherless wings still on my back, and I looked to the sky, towards that sun that I had become, towards that goal that I will never shake, towards my own recognition of Limitlessness.

Part I
Fastening the Wings

A sure method must be elucidated on the matter of self-godhood and its attainment. The trickeries of sorcery and devotions of mysticism are but paths to the same palace, but ritual and prayer must be set aside and a straight line must be drawn from one point to another.

From my journal of metaphysical experimentations, in a conversation with the Aeon of Ra: "Remember the words, 'Hael Mah Tankel,' 'I Am the Path.' You are the Path, and the Palace at the end of the Path. You know all things, you simply need to remember them."

You are the Path, and the Palace at the end of the Path. You are the seeker, and you are that which is sought, and you are the journey between the two.

The years between my parting from the methods of occultism, especially its more sinister manifestations, and the present were spent largely in a grand experiment in my own godhood. Guided by gurus, Spiritual Masters, and the spiritual entities that I was able to call upon, I learned a great many truths about my nature as an Eternal being, a Limitless identity - a God. First among these is the solidity of that reality, the unwavering certainty that I am, just as all beings are, God. And that, as a conscious nexion, the individual is capable of consciously experiencing his own godhood. Not only is he capable, but it is his ultimate destiny, it is the unwhispered thing that drives him forward and upwards in his experiences of incarnation. This truth, the understanding of this truth, does not come by study or by intellectual contemplation, or by faith or acceptance of the unthinkable, but by experience. "The more you act as supreme architect, the more you become one."[1] Conversely, the more often you become the supreme architect, the more you will act like one, and the greater your conscious experience as such will become.

All other realizations that I had, and that anyone can have other than this primary one, constitute the method of attaining a more concrete realization of the first, adding upon it in depth and girth. The surety of those methods is recognized when the fruits that they offer are consistent, and their results are reproducible.

All religions have struggled to teach what is herein so plainly laid out. All messiahs have tried and often died to shed light on this simple guide. Every science, esoteric and mundane, has as their unspoken goal the very immortality and limitless potency that these works unveil.

None of this is new, however. It has simply been forgotten.

Chapter One
Feathers to Fly

Tucked deep inside the warmth of my mother's body, her safety keeping me safe, her nourishment feeding me, I could sense that she was powerless. She wanted with all of her will to hold me, to love me, to raise me as best she could, but the circumstances in her life would not relent. She was powerless. And I felt it too, a crushing weight like the deepest waters, suffocating and threatening to implode my frail body.

Powerless.

For months I felt it growing slowly, my descent into the oceanic abyss traveled by the inch, one inch every day for months, compressing me with the monstrous force of powerlessness. Her fear kept me afraid. Her doubt made my conviction in the ability to surmount a tyrannical reality buckle. Her powerlessness became mine, inherited like her blond hair and hazel eyes, swallowed into my body as if fed through our shared umbilical cord.

Then I saw her, in the blinding light and blurred, wet canvas of an open world, I saw her. Her love and pride, still sensed although I was no longer inside of her, were drowned out by the sure and unrelenting knowledge that she could not take on the mantle of the Mother. She tried, for months more, to defy destiny and to be reborn as a demigod capable of the miraculous, but powerlessness prevailed.

A man with power, a Father too, offered to take this burden from her, and he did. The power that he held, however, was far too much for him to absorb and assimilate, and so as it spilled out onto the floor beneath him it soaked his being, his soul wicking up the wet upon his feet, sickening him with spiritual pneumonia. He refused to be a powerless one, however, and so he continued to invoke the untamable power. Children were the siphon into which he would drain his overflow. He had several siphons, some of them his and some collected on his journey, but as they sickened from the onslaught of overflow that he forced into them and as they became weaker and less capable to relieve his own torment, the gods that he worshipped sent him me, his final siphon.

I was still too small when he collected me, still too frail to feed his sickness into me, and so he waited, and as he did all of the other powerless siphons clung to me, the unsoiled filter, as a hope for purity and light and love.

One day this man who overflowed with power burst from the flood of it, taking on the role of Caine and slaying his righteous and upright brother who demanded that his sacrifices to God be pure. The power had taken him, and as his sin was discovered and he was put into chains, he too realized that he was powerless.

The government was confused with what to do with several broken siphons and one unused one, lying in my bare crib covered in feces, bones showing through my skin. I went here and there and to other places, other homes, with children who were not broken at all – who in fact had never even been used! I was confused, but I was comforted by the knowledge of the one constant upon which I could rely, and I waited for powerlessness again to cradle me in its arms.

A boy watching television on a Wednesday night saw me on a program, although I don't recall being filmed. He had four sisters, none of whom wanted to make bows and arrows out of willow trees or to build forts from straw and sticks. He called on his parents to see me on the television, because he was sure that I was to be his brother.

When they came to collect me and my two black garbage bags and one small suitcase filled with my belongings, the man who would become my father smiled. He was a big man, tall with strong arms, broad shoulders, and a gigantic smile. I don't know that I've seen him smile that big since.

They had a large house with plenty of rooms, and my own bed on the bottom of a bunk in my new brother's bedroom. I wasn't able to cross midline, meaning that my right hand could not interact with objects on the left side of my body, and the reverse, due to the lack of three-dimensional objects in my four years of development. So, until that was corrected, I slept on the bottom bunk.

My new mother started taking me to a school where I learned a little bit of simple sign language like "butterfly" and "rhinoceros," as well as speaking, recognizing shapes, and mastering balance. I was never sure why I had to go to this school when my new sister, only a year younger than I, stayed at home and played, but I was told to, and so I did.

It was one day when, unaided, I walked the entire length of a balance beam that I understood that I was learning not how to walk, talk, or play, but I was learning the secrets through which I could gain conscious and precise power over my own body.

Power wasn't given to me by fact, but instead was learned, suffered for, and eventually earned through discipline.

I was always the type of person, even as a child, that when I had learned something that to me was new and perhaps for me revolutionary, I would run and tell the whole world what I had learned, thrilling in explaining and illustrating and pantomiming and doing whatever it took to communicate both the essence and the importance of the thing to my sometimes quite literally captive audience. That has never changed.

When I was twelve and began experimenting with the occult and studying medieval witchcraft and the knowledge of substantial spiritual contact solidified into reality, this curious attribute was magnified. At sixteen years old, I had formed my first occult Circle, and at seventeen my first coven.

After years of struggling with the various occult disciplines aimed at viewing with opened eyes anything of spiritual substance, at leaving my body with full conscious recollection of the events, and of commanding the energies around me to physical phenomenon, and experienced quite a bit of success at all junctures, I still needed more. I turned to the religion of my upbringing, the Church of Jesus Christ of Latter-Day Saints, in hopes that combining my occult disciplines with a religion which purported to offer godhood – which had always been my ultimate goal - I would finally unlock its mysteries. I was met with sheer disappointment. A year into my membership in the church, and a marital engagement to one of their greatest disciples, I was introduced to a man who would forever alter my path, who seemed to be Destiny Incarnate. This man appeared to me, not in a crowded restaurant or a busy street, but *appeared* to me in the center of my locked bedroom, where I was reading from various religious texts, the Rig Vegas being chief among them.

"The path is cleared now," he said. "All waters have been made aright." And then he vanished, the body that had seemed so solid and corporeal simply dissipated before me into nothingness.

I, too, had learned various methods of astral projection, soul travel, bilocation, and remote viewing, although I had never been able to solidify my presence with such a critical mass as to appear physically present. And so I followed the spiritual stranger, focusing my soul's attention on his face, his dark skinned, beard covered face. My body seemed to tremble and gyrate back and forth, my equilibrium completely lost in the leaving, the floor dropping out from beneath me to reveal the absence of anything that reality sits upon, my head spinning to the point where my feet previously were, and then to the side. Through the control of my breath, steadily in and out, I stabilized my motion and moved upwards and out. The cities and continents passed by me and I found myself at a cold, yet very green mountain, soaring up the mountain, through the trees, on a side of it that seemed to be entirely hidden from the ventures of any physical traveler. On that hidden side of the mountain, which the sun seemed to illuminate all of the time, there sat a temple, a ziggurat to be precise, and on the large steps of its structure sat dozens of robed disciples laying and sitting and relaxed in tranced meditation.

One of them noticed me and announced, "Sri Suhnam will only see you if you are invited."

"He has already seen me," I prodded.

The disciple did not appear amused at my wordplay, and reiterated, "No one is allowed to enter the Temple without permission."

That sounded more like a challenge than anything else, and so I left the steps of the ziggurat and moved through the stones that composed it to find myself in a tremendously open space, at the center of it stood a large pedestal upon which a book was placed, opened, the pages of which appeared to be manufactured of gold leafs. And the man, the Master, Suhnam, stood behind the pulpit reading to himself, the whole of his congregation outside, seeming to be hearing his very thoughts as he silently read. I hovered in my spiritual body behind him to catch a glimpse of the book, and in that same instant, he slammed it shut and swiveled his head around to see me, looking me directly in the eyes. I had never before been so startled, that a person in a seeming body of flesh would not only see my incorporeal visage, but could look me in the eyes with such parental scorn.

"You can return tomorrow," his rough and tired voice scolded, "and I will read the book to you."

I immediately opened my eyes and was back inside of my body, either the terror of the my spying revealed thrusting me back, or a sort of sending-away from the Siddha upon whom I had spied forcing me back into my form.

I had soul traveled before. I had astral projected. I had moved across space in a nonphysical body to observe the activities of others, but never had I penetrated into such a secret and sacred place, and never had I been observed observing. Furthermore, never had I had contact with such a powerful entity, in all of my evocations, visions, and visitations. When Suhnam had vanished from my bedroom, I assumed that I could play the same game as he. I learned in the minutes of my travel to his temple, however, that we were not playing the same game at all. I understood that only *I* was playing the game... a game that he had already won and was done with.

I could not speak a word for the remainder of the day.

When I awoke the next morning, I rose from my bed, and without brushing my teeth or eating breakfast, without even a morning cigarette, I took a seat in a chair I had placed in the corner of my bedroom, closed my eyes, and prepared myself for the psychic maelstrom that accompanied leaving my body. I was pleasantly disappointed. The imbalance that needed to be battled against in order to leave myself was gone, and in the moment that my eyes were closed and my intention was set, I was on the steps of Suhnam's temple. I no longer wore the boxer shorts and tank top that I had dressed myself in, but instead was in a drab, tan robe, sitting with the many disciples on the steps, surrounding Suhnam

He began to read from this book, although his eyes never glanced at the pages. It was as if the words that he spoke mutated once they struck the air, or once they struck our ears, however, changing into the words that each disciple needed to hear.

"You must find balance in all things," he read to me. "You are in constant conflict. 'Should I do this? Should I do that? What will people think of me? What will I have to sacrifice?' You ask yourself ten thousand questions, yet you arrive not with answers, but with more questions. Cease the questions. Care not about the answers. Simply BE. Your Dharma is already set, the river is already flowing. Fighting your Dharma is a state of stagnancy. Allowing the river to take you where it will is the only motion that is real."

As he continued to read, on and on for what seemed like hours, the words jumbled and then faded, and became one stream of thought, of emotion, of light and wisdom, transferred directly from the reader and the book into the listener, into me. I then knew the trance that his other disciples were under, as the same blank look was then in my eyes.

When the reading seemed to stop and the whole congregation sat in a stupor of love and peace, my curiosity broke the spell and I spoke to the Master.

"Suhnam, is anyone here physically?"

"We are all here, and this is a physical place, yes," he answered with infinite patience.

"But, I mean, my body isn't here. It's sitting in a chair in my bedroom, so I'm not physically here."

"But you are here, are you not?" he asked.

"Well, I am here, but not physically."

"Is there a difference?"

To me there was a huge difference, an immense difference, a catastrophic difference. If I could bring my body to this Temple and meet in the flesh with such a Master, it would be all the more real to me. There would be no doubt upon my return to the flesh, as there always seemed to be.

Suhnam chuckled to himself. "There are levels of discipline that you must attain, and if you would prefer to begin your discipline with one whose understanding is limited as yours is, I will send you one. This world is filled with those who are on the edge of realization, as you are, and so connecting the two should be no task at all."

With another chuckle from the Master, I was returned to my body.

At some point in the week following, I visited my friend, Jason, at his request. Upon arriving however, his mother seemed much more intent on talking to me than Jason did. We sat in her front room on white couches with pink embroidered flowers, and she told me about a Hindu mystic that she had just met, and she had experienced a dream in which this mystic, Baba Maharaja, had instructed her to find me and bring me to him.

My studies in the occult in general were beginning to wane, as I found that once the basics of evocation, candle magick, sigil drawing, and the like were learned, the only depth that remained was self-created. I was in search instead for a vacuum of experience from which I could not escape, a bottomless rabbit hole... the annunciation that would cause of all known reality to crumble and reveal the Kingdom of Heaven all around me.

But the thought of a Hindu mystic and all of my xenophobic conceptions of a turban-wearing cab driver pointing me towards absolution wasn't helped by the fact that Wendy, Jason's mother, continued to refer to him as a "Yogi."

I had met with self-proclaimed embodied-demons, had evoked more spirits than I could enumerate, had studied, meditated, and prayed with just about every spiritual group I could find, and so I could find no justification for rejecting an outright offer to meet a "mystic."

A tall, muscular man opened the apartment door. His black hair was long and curly, and his neatly trimmed black beard contrasted against his dark skin and baby blue eyes. There was no way that this guy could be from India. More striking, however, was the envelope of peace that surrounded him, a strong and forceful peace that swept out before him and buzzed through his apartment. Upon shaking my hand, he looked into my eyes and stated, "We've met before."

"No," I replied. "I don't live in Vegas anymore."

He laughed. "Not from here." He looked at me more intently. "Yes, that's right, we met in the Temple. You'll remember."

I stood in my place, not knowing what to say. "Well, I'm Baba Maharaja, but my friends call me Raj." Raj directed us into his apartment and asked us to sit on his couch.

"So, Wendy told me that you've been dabbling in witchcraft, is that right?"

"Yeah," I affirmed. "But not really dabbling. I mean, I'm not just playing games with it. I know what I'm doing."

"Of course you do." Again, he smiled, like a parent to an annoyed child. "But you're looking for something more, now? You have a path of discipline ahead of you, and you are ready to begin on that path, otherwise you would not have come here."

"That's a possibility," I answered.

"But what I'd like to do today," Raj continued, ignoring my skepticism, "is help you get your energy straightened out, and see if I can help you get you into balance. There is much work to be done, but it can't be approached with this sort of turmoil in and around you."

"Okay."

"Now, I've been studying spirituality my whole life as well, and I've learned how to see the energy that is around people. It helps me know how I can help them. Right now I can see your charkas. Do you know what chakras are?"

"Yep," I answered, happy to finally feel engaged in the conversation I was having. "They're the energy centers in the astral body. They all have different colors and are connected to different organs or glands in the physical body."

"Well, you've got the base of it," Raj said. "The word 'chakra' actually means 'disk.' Your chakras are bright, colored disks of light floating just off of your skin. If you tune in to your Ajna Chakra, or your Third Eye, you'll start to see energy, and will learn how to see auras and chakras, and even spiritual beings that aren't here physically. You'll also be able to purify anything in your life, and to bring anything into your life that you desire. Like Shiva, all of the power in this world lies in the Ajna Chakra."

"Cool," I said, amazed at what could be waiting for me if I continued down this antisocial path of spiritual realization.

"Yeah, it is pretty cool," Raj said with a smile. "Right now I can see that you have a few chakras that aren't quite moving the right way, and your Solar Plexus is a lot stronger than the others, which could be causing an imbalance in the rest of your chakras. Would you mind lying on my floor?"

Confused as to what was going to happen, I laid on the floor. Raj lit some incense and turned his CD player on, filling the room with soft music and spiraling smoke. He held a crystal, suspended by a silver chain, over my body, inches off of my skin. As he moved the crystal in the air from my head to my feet, the crystal would visibly jump, pull, or even spin as it hovered over certain parts of my body. Raj put the crystal away, asked me to close my eyes, and began moving his hands over my body, not touching me but creating a noticeable magnetic effect wherever his hands moved to. As his hands passed over me again and again, he began to chant in an unknown language, and the sound of it put me into a deep sleep.

I awoke to see Baba Maharaja's sparkling eyes. "You got pretty relaxed, huh," he said, laughing. "I've balanced out your chakras for now, but it's going to be up to you to keep them that way. You seem like you're able to get your hands on information pretty easily, so see if you can find some good information on opening your chakras."

"Okay," I said, not sure if this was the disappointing end to our visit.

"I have a couple of exercises for you to do," he told me. He showed me a few basic yoga postures, calling them the pyramid, the cobra, and the samurai – names that I have yet to hear again in reference to yogic asanas, despite years of study and practice of the system. Raj instructed me to do these daily.

During the pyramid I was to breathe deeply, with each inhalation gathering up all of my anger and emotion, and with the following exhalation to send this energy down my arms and legs, into the ground.

Once no more emotion could be exhausted, I was to move into the cobra position, clearing myself of all thought.

Finally, I was to move into the samurai posture, create a vision in my mind of what I'd like my world to be like, to raise my arms above my head, clasping my fingers together, forming a steeple out of my index fingers, and sending my vision into a ray of bright light out of my fingers and into the world.

We sat together in the samurai pose, facing one another, and he guided me through the visualization, telling me to imagine any situation in my life, and to begin to change it in my inner to the way I'd like it to be. I visualized a relationship with a family member that had been sour for years, and could feel the knots in my stomach and the tightness in my chest as I brought to mind the negative. I then erased that image and brought to mind an ideal relationship with this person, a loving and respectful friendship. My entire body relaxed, and I could feel my spine straightening and a force barely rambling my shoulders and my arms and the tips of my fingers as the pure will for peace was generated in my body. On Raj's direction, I released these thoughts through my fingers on waves of light, across the miles of desert towards my goal.

"You see," Raj said. "Once you can balance your thoughts, once you can make peace within yourself, you can do the same to the whole world around you."

I was speechless. For years I had been lighting candles and singing incantations, drawing symbols on paper or in the dirt, begging the forces of the occult to aid me, yet here, in the space of an hour I was learning that I was the central power, that I was the manifestor of my own destiny, not through external rituals, but through an alteration of the internal state, which would then be reflected in the physical world.

"Can you stay a while longer?" Raj asked, his eyes pleading with me.

"Sure," I said, although I felt as if my cup was already full and was about to overflow.

"How long will you be able to stay?" he asked. "One month? Maybe three?"

"I have a job I have to go to Monday morning," I protested. "I have an apartment and roommates and a life. I can't just disappear for three months."

Again, he smiled. "Your job, do you want to stay there for the rest of your life?"

"Well, no."

"And your roommates, will their lives be interrupted or disturbed by your absence?"

"They would miss me, I think," I said.

"You do have a long road ahead of you," he reiterated. "You must become the Warrior and the Priest before you can become the Wizard." Whatever that meant.

The idea of leaving my life for only a few months terrified me, but the glow of sanctity within his home felt like a womb that I would never want to leave.

I knelt in the samurai posture, facing Raj who did the same, and together we raised our arms above our heads, clasped our hands to form two steeples, and with the exhalation of our breath, aligned the physical world to our intentions.

I asked to use his telephone and called my employer, telling him that I had an emergency arise which would require my absence for three months.

"Alright, buddy," my boss said without a quiver. "Whatever you need. Just let me know when you're ready to come back, and your job will be waiting."

My roommates were just as nonchalant to hold my apartment room for me while I left, paying my portion of the rent until I returned.

"You will never have to worry about money, food, clothing, or any of the other things of this world," Raj informed me. "When you are at peace and in balance, all of these things will come to you. In fact, the less you want them, the less you seek after them, the more they will be laid at your doorstep."

I slept on a bearskin rug in his living room. He offered me a spare bed, but the rug was much more comfortable. I awoke in the morning not to the sound of his voice, but to a soft voice, a woman's voice.

"Wake up, precious one," she said. As the blurriness left my eyes, I saw a beautiful, blonde, thin woman standing above me. "You have a lot of work to do today, I'm sure. I'll see you tonight."

I stood and rubbed my eyes, a little embarrassed about my morning-messy hair and the disheveled clothes I had slept in, but I noticed that she did not notice. She hugged and kissed Raj goodbye, and then turned to me with her arms out. I had never met this woman before, but she possessed the same remarkable spiritual radiance as Raj, and as I hugged her I melted into her, no rousing of the sexual impulses or misplaced emotions that I had expected, but a feeling of absolute peace. This woman, Raj's mate, would come and go, but seemed to not linger long at all, never interrupting our work and never giving me the chance to get to know her at all.

Raj invited me to bathe and change into "something comfortable" while he prepared breakfast. I noticed, along with his obviously expensive towels and cloths, that he did not have a shower, but only a bath. I hadn't taken a bath, an actual bath, since I was a child, but I knew that after my drive to Las Vegas and my day spent in the summer heat of that city that I needed to bathe.

The "comfortable clothing" that I chose were a pair of jeans and a t-shirt with a rock band logo on the front. He laughed as I emerged from the bathroom, and said that after breakfast we would need to go shopping. I protested, as I was inclined to do so often, that I didn't have much money to buy a new wardrobe.

"Don't worry about it," he assured me. "I have plenty of money."

"I can't let you buy me things with *your* money," I insisted.

"It's not *my* money," he said with a smile. "People just give it to me, and I do what I can to give them what I am able. It's all a cycle."

Raj appeared to be unaffected in any way by the world around him, by the mostly-nude women on posters and taxis through the city, by the noise of honking horns and shouting voices, by the prostitutes and drug addicts in the center of the city. He wore a smile on his lips and a glimmer in his eyes like a child seeing the world for the first time, and not the least bit offended by any of it.

Along with various incenses and oils, Raj purchased a few pairs of loose, white, cotton pants for me, and was very specific about buying a large, indigo candle. He had to find one that was indigo rather than a simple blue.

When I re-emerged from his bathroom wearing the loose, white pants and a white tank top, Raj smiled and said, "Let's begin!"

He instructed me to enter the "pyramid" posture, with my hands and feet flat on the floor, my body facing downwards, and my waist pulled up towards the ceiling, making a triangle of my body. In modern, westernized yoga, this is called the "downward facing dog." In Sanskrit, it is called "Adho Mukha Svanasana," which in fact does translate to "downward facing dog posture." Raj preferred to call this the pyramid, because the root emotional and energy centers, the Muladhara Chakra, the Swadisthana Chakra, and the Manipura Chakra, are those that are generally responsible for negative emotions and energies, and therefore needed to be raised above the others and allowed to drain of their negativity before continuing.

With deep breaths, I could feel the fire within me, within these centers, within the peak of my body's pyramid churning. Emotions of my childhood, my parents, past relationships, present circumstances, and every other negative or counterproductive emotion and thought would arise, and as I exhaled, I could physically feel these draining down my arms and my legs. My breathing became more furious as more emotions arose, and rather than the position and the breathing wearing my body down, it energized me with the rising rage and its gradual dissipation.

After several minutes of this, Raj instructed me to enter the Cobra, with legs kicked out, flat on the ground behind me, my hand on the ground beneath my shoulders, the strength of my arms lifting my torso up off of the ground, my eyes cast towards the ceiling, a posture known in yoga as "Urdvha Mukha Svanasana," or "Upwards Facing Dog Posture." My breaths here were cool and relaxing, the energy flowing down from the universe into my Ajna Chakra, which was pointed upwards, and distilling down into all of my lower chakras. This posture counteracted the previous one, calming my emotions, clarifying my mind, and bringing my body into relaxation.

And then I moved into the Samurai, kneeling with my knees apart, my buttocks resting on my heels, my shoulders back and my chest open, and my hands relaxed on my knees. Raj sat in the position with me, and together we raised our arms into steeples.

"What will we be changing?" I asked, as my introduction into this posture was one of altering reality through the discharge of energy.

"Only ourselves," Raj said. "If you are always trying to change the world around you, then you do not live in the true space, which is within. The world is perfect, as it is a reflection of yourself. If you don't like what you see in the world, then all that you can do is to change the way that you see it, and the world will reflect a different image for you."

The room grew visibly brighter as we focused on bringing spiritual light into our beings, and when we lowered our hands to our sides, slowly, pulling the energy with us back to the earth, the peace was overwhelming. We sat perhaps for hours simply breathing the peace and the love into ourselves, and breathing the peace and love back out.

These basic yoga sessions, consisting of only the three asanas, followed by a period of pranayama, or "control of breath/control of life force," lasted for hours, taking up most of the day. As the scorching Las Vegas sun set, the streets cooled down, the rushing cars diminished, and the noise grew to a reasonable hum, Raj and I would go for a walk. He called this a "Walking Meditation," the idea of which was to maintain the same state of tranquility, of serenity, of unity, while moving about in the world.

"Most disciplines will have you perform your Walking Meditation in a garden or temple or some other serene place," Raj told me as we descended the concrete steps from his apartment onto the streets. "I have chosen this city, and this area, for a reason. It requires little discipline to be at peace, to be nonattached, when you are in a peaceful place. But to walk through these streets, as God in the flesh, with the light of Divinity in your veins and a love for everything in your heart, with a clear mind, while people try to sell you sex or poisons of every kind, with a million things that could distract your focus... that requires real discipline. But once you have it, once you are disciplined in such a way, you can be in perfect peace and love while witnessing the horrors of these lower worlds. You can be in perfect peace in the face of murder or genocide. You are in this world, not of it. You cannot be attached to these things that are passing, but only to that which is Eternal."

We walked for at least an hour each day, our eyes not looking at the world around us, but looking *through* the world around us, seeing the flow of the spiritual everywhere, in everything, in every casino, in every liquor store, in every prostitute and drunk and homeless person. Seeing God in all things. The reflections off of the glass buildings and the sun soaking into the black, tar-snaked pavement, all of the colors and sights and sounds and smells wafting through the city became an overwhelming ecstasy of sensory experience. And I was never to yield, neither to the distractions of the world around us nor to the climax of the senses as the spiritual and the physical collided between us.

Raj could sense immediately when I would become distracted, when my eyes would refocus on the material world. He could feel the horror returning to me, and would remind me gently to return my attention that that which was real, not that which *appeared* to be real.

After one month of the same basic discipline, Raj decided that I was ready for another level. Following the period of asanas and pranayama, he lit the indigo candle on a small table. With my mind empty, my heart pure, my body calmed, and my senses attuned, Raj instructed me to gaze into the flame of the candle. This was nothing new for me, like a simple candle-magick exercise that I played with when I was a teenager.

I gazed into the flame and breathed, and could feel the indigo energy enveloping the fire. Just as I thought that the exercise was going perfectly, Raj added the instruction, "Don't blink!"

My eyes spun away from the candle towards my mentor. "Don't *blink*?"

"Don't blink," he said again, his tone not changing or wavering, no explanation to follow.

The candle's flame scorched my watering eyes, tears streaming down my cheeks, every muscle in my body clenching and shaking, trying to force my leaden eyelids from closing. My first attempt yielded one minute of success. I'm certain that I had not blinked my eyes for longer than a minute before, but to do so *consciously* was the real trick.

The feat exhausted me, my skin dripping sweat as if I had just sprinted ten miles, all of my willpower, my physical and mental strength, pushed towards the single and simple goal of looking at the flame of a candle without blinking.

Raj felt my aggravation and he could sense my feeling of failure, as well as my utter desire to give up the task altogether.

"Start with two minutes," he told me, his voice more gentle than I remember it ever being before. "And then every day, add another thirty seconds, and soon ten minutes will pass without a blink, without even a temptation, and you will be ready to leave here."

Mastery over this exercise, in combination with all of the others, was the key to the gate that would begin my journey into the spiritual realm, into the full Mastery of the Self. As I sat each day with the candle lit before me, Raj would stand behind me and to the right, and I would hear his voice over my shoulder, whispering additional instructions.

"Relax your body... your chest has become tight. Don't forget to breathe."

When I had reached a glorious five-minute mark, he began what seemed to me to be the real instruction.

"Breathe in, and pull the indigo light from the flame into your Ajna Chakra. Breathe out and let that light float downwards, through all of your chakras, but specifically into your Manipura Chakra, in your stomach, where your most violent and powerful emotions are stored. Continue doing this, breathing the indigo light in, which is Agni, the fire of purification, Shiva's light, and using it to purify your Manipura Chakra, and you will find that all other chakras become balanced, and your body becomes balanced, your mind becomes balanced, and then all things around you become balanced."

The magick of the practice began opening up to me. I could feel my Third Eye prying itself wider, the lights and sounds from the other side rushing in at me. The burning in my eyes and the tears running down my face no longer effected me, no longer made me wince. All that mattered was the indigo light and the candle's flame.

Once I had reached the ten-minute mark, I inhaled deeply, and heard Raj's voice whisper, "As you let that breath out, give the word, 'Soham Akaal.' Immortality of the Soul."

I let the breath out and my voice vibrated, "SOHAM AKAAL."

The rushing winds that the crack between the worlds seemed to cause were silenced, the fury of the indigo flame burning through my body was made still, and for a single moment all that I knew was that I was God.

Chapter Two
Immutable Wax

Raj's "Blue Flame Meditation," as he called it, not only opened my vision to the spiritual currents and forces around me, and indeed around and within all things, but it also brought my mind into extreme clarity and focus, to the degree that I began to develop a sort of "photographic memory." I hesitate to strictly describe this new sort of memory awareness as photographic, specifically, because it was not as if my mind was taking a photograph of what I had seen and capturing the still image in some psychic memory bank. It was instead as if the *spirit* of the thing was absorbed into all three of my eyes, understood intimately, and recalled easily like an old lover. Through this method of enhanced memory, I was able to look at pages of a book, flipping through them, absorbing the spirit of each page, and was able to present an accurate synopsis of the general plot, although a good deal of the details that make such readings enjoyable were lost. What was interesting to me, however, was that the *emotion* that would be conveyed in those details was the sharpest aspect of the whole experience. I would flip through chapters of a book in seconds, and looking up from the pages would find my eyes filled with tears, sobbing for the plight of the characters described.

My mind was a ready siphon for all information that it touched, the light within everything radiating with such vibrancy and clarity that like Raj, I too looked at the world like a new and amazed child.

Like Shiva, however, I was not content to simply sit in silent meditation and receive. I could hear Maharaja's instruction and was ready to open my Ajna Chakra not to receive, but to transmit, to assert my will upon the worlds, the physical and those beyond the five senses. I had learned that the words "Soham Akaal" did not simply mean "Immortality of the Soul," as Raj had told me, coating the powerful mantra with honey as he had. Soham is the self, the ever-present "I," ego, the "I AM" principle which is the necessary ego-attachment for every spiritual manifestor and Sorcerer to make substantial alterations in reality without the use of physical force. Coupled with the word, "Akaal," which does not only mean "immortal," but also denotes "Eternal, limitless, boundless," and "Supreme," the mantra invokes the grand formula of, "I Am God." With each repetition of that ritual every day the force that was building in me was unstoppable. The information that I was absorbing into my brain was overwhelming, but was leading me towards a clear realization of the processes required to sublimate the weakest and dying parts of myself and to immortalize that within me which did realize in those moments at the climax of my meditations that I am God. A clear path was laid out for me, a map that I would follow that would bring me into absolute Mastery over the Self.

Daily Meditation

Raj had not only taught me the value of meditation each and every day, regardless of physical ailment or emotional duress, but also that meditation has three stages, and all three need to be entered into, acknowledged, and passed through.

The first stage in the meditative process is the Climb. Even if you have been successfully meditating for most of your life, there is still a physical and physiological adjustment period when you relax your muscles, allow your heart-rate to decelerate, purge your mind of the anxieties of life, and settle into a comfortable pattern of breathing. This climbing phase is most awkward when first learning to meditate, or when returning to the practice of daily meditation after a lengthy break in the discipline.

Trying to "astral project" when I was sixteen, sleeping over at a friend's house, we both laid on the floor on our backs, closed our eyes, relaxed our bodies, and tried to imagine leaving ourselves. I had read in some New Age guide to astral projection that if you are able to imagine yourself as some object other than that which you are, such as a flower, and fully become that other object, that the act of astral projection would occur quite automatically. I imagined a rose, the stem lightly bending, the tips of the leaves beginning to brown against the crisp, green leaf, the petals in the beginning stages of unraveling. I then imagined myself inside of the rose, my legs becoming the stem, my arms the leaves, and my shoulders, neck, and head becoming the flower itself. Just as the whole imagined process neared a critical mass where my identity as a human animal faded and a new identity as a rose took its place, I felt as if the floor had dropped out from underneath me. My legs and arms fell through the floor, and the rest of my body seemed to be spinning in the vacuous space that once was my friend's bedroom. The spinning was nauseating, not simply because I was moving in circles, but more because my body seemed to be spinning in every direction at once. I shot my eyelids open and my fingers scratched to hold onto the fibers of the carpet, to stabilize myself in this world. It took me several minutes to convince myself that I was once again in a concrete world.

And then it came to my attention that my friend had had the exact same experience.

We had both heard the urban legend of some kid, about our age, not far from where we lived, who astral projected and got "stuck" outside of his body. He was put in a hospital, so said the legend, where he still remains, comatose, still trying to reunite flesh and spirit. We wondered out loud to each other if we had come close to experiencing such a terrifying event and were saved at the last minute by the grace of God – or some other powerful entity.

Years later, thinking back on this, it is absurdly obvious that: 1. While the visualization of the rose and the merging of the self with that object is a great tool for meditation, and even for the practices potentially leading to Samadhi, it is not at all relevant to the practice of astral projection; 2. That what we had experienced was the aforementioned physiological adjustment taking place, combined with a certain psychic unsteadiness that needed to be brought into balance in order to glide into the Theta brainwave state; and 3. That no such person exists trapped outside of their comatose body.

I still have a similar experience when I have events or struggles appear in my life that take me away from my practice of daily meditation or from all spiritual practices, which is the case every so often. When I have finally surpassed the ordeal and am ready to return to a life of living "in the spirit," I'll get out of bed an hour early, get dressed and ready for the day, move around the house a bit to get my blood flow balanced, and then I'll sit in a chair, let my eyes drift shut, and turn my attention towards my breath. Almost immediately I will be hit with a dizziness and loss of equilibrium; it is through nothing but willpower that I am able to complete the meditation. Nearly every time this occurs, that first day of my return into the spirit fills me with the most extreme frustration, disappointment, and doubt.

Perhaps I'm just not capable of meditating anymore. Maybe I'm not able to get into touch with my inner self, and with the Eternal power around and within me. Maybe I'm doomed to be trapped as nothing more than a physical being for the rest of my days.

On the second day, I'll wake up, my feet dragging a bit more than the previous morning, dreading a repeat of the substandard meditation, but when I sit and turn my attention inwards, and the fullness of my focus turns towards my breath, there is no dizziness, no confusion, no fuzzy lack of balance.

Each breath pulls me deeper within myself, and as I breathe out, my consciousness expands infinitely into the universe, and once again I know the bliss of being in spirit.

Whether you are sitting down to meditate for the first time, or if you are competent in entering higher and deeper mindstates at will, you are still bound by the need to relax your body and your thoughts and to move your consciousness deeper within. The only difference between the neophyte and the adept in this regard is that the adept is able to move through this process much more quickly, and he does not mentally berate himself for the necessity of the process – the latter virtue greatly contributing to the former.

The second stage of meditating, the Climax, much like its obvious sexual counterpart, is often the most elusive and fleeting of the three stages. During the Climbing stage, there is a definite struggle, a battle to keep the attention off of the body and its environment, and focused singly upon the breath, the rising and falling of the subtle energetic states, and the achievement of that glorious spiritual crescendo.

In the twinkling of an eye, the struggle is given up, the mind forfeiting the battle. Bliss descends from the ether and in an instant overwhelms every cell in your body, the buzzing excitement expanding beyond the skin and seeming to illuminate the room.

And just as you think to yourself, "Ah, I've *finally* done it!" you have once again lost it. Mind has won, ego asserting its power and ejecting every ounce of grace from your being.

Unless a person is properly disciplined in various Shaivistic and Tantric practices which will allow the spiritual union of the sexual experience to override the purely genital reactions to intercourse, the sexual encounter and the struggle towards orgasm is restricted by sensitivity and physiology. The orgasm of the soul is incarcerated by no such restrictions. The neophyte to meditation will take offense at his apparent failure and will attempt to take revenge on his perceived enemy, his mind. Squinting his eyes shut and stiffening his lips, he will breathe even deeper and harder and will lock his mind even more resolutely on his goal of liberation. He will eventually succeed, but only after exhaustion sets in and he becomes again lost in his breath, and once he forgets his goal and simply embraces it.

The adept, when he realizes that he has spent himself, will smile, sometimes laugh, and will gracefully re-enter the mystical experience and bathe in the ever-flowing waters of life.

The final stage, which is the reason for the joy of the adept's failure, I have called the Afterglow. Once the meditative state has been passed through and the Climax has subsided, a unique inner quietude and satisfaction warms the whole being. Initially, it is required to quiet the mind and contemplate the whole ordeal in order to really notice the Afterglow, as frustrations about the "failure" of the meditation or longings to return to the meditative state will overwhelm the satisfaction of the moment. Often, the Afterglow itself is more emotionally and psychically fulfilling than the Climax, the whole being still stretched into infinity, the mind lingering between the worlds.

Following my study with Baba Maharaja, I again met with Master Suhnam to resume my studies in my own Ascent. My meditative state had solidified and my spiritual bodies seemed to be gaining prevalence over even my physical body and mind, to the extent that projection of my mind outside of my body and into higher states of consciousness and planes of existence was primary rather than secondary nature.

Suhnam guided me out of my body, through the astral plane, the causal realm, the mental realm, across a dark region of spirituality often referred to as the "abyss," and into a realm that I can only refer to as the "formative plane," as there are no embodiments, no thoughts, nothing that is formed, but simply liquid color, light, and sound. I became the light that rushed by me, melting into the pool of power, losing all consciousness of self, not concerned with form or even with the analysis of the experience, but lost in the bliss of being and not being in the same moment.

When I recollected my ego, my identity, and returned to the flesh, my whole body sparkled with the intense bliss, and I wore a smile that I just couldn't shake. I felt as if I had not fully returned to my body, but that a part of me still lingered in that formative plane. For the first three days I understood the state of nonattachment that the Masters have always spoken of: no matter what happened, no matter who cut me off while driving or the dirty looks I received for my permanent smile, regardless of the daily frustrations of life, everything was perfect. At some point during the fourth day, however, the experience started to annoy me. I felt like I could not ground myself, that I could not bring myself back to "reality" – the physical reality that my body and mind was familiar with. I turned on the most vulgar music I could think of, but the only sound that my mind could process was the buzzing of the power in that plane. I ate the most unhealthy food I could find, trying to put enough weight and fat on my soul to bring it back to earth, but that unseen part of me remained in between. Most irritating, I even tried to drown the elation with alcohol, but the drug seemed to have no effect on me at all. A stack of hamburgers, a pile of metal and rap CDs, and a half a bottle of Jack Daniels later, I gave up.

I awoke the next morning, and the afterglow had ended. And I could feel my heart drop. Being completely happy, content, and at peace was so alien to me at that point in my life that I did all that I could to reject it. And for the time being, it was "the one that got away."

Chapter Three
The Silver Harness

The experience of trying to merge my identity with that of a flower on my friend's carpeted floor was only the first of many failed attempts at projecting my consciousness outside of my body.

Traveling outside of the fleshy prison had been, since I had first heard of the possibility, one of my chief goals in my application of practical spirituality. I followed the instructions given in every New Age book I could find on the subject, and was able to visualize myself leaving my body, I could imagine the sights and sounds with perfect clarity. But none of it seemed to extend any further than my imagination. My consciousness was still trapped inside of my brain and was still restricted by the chemical ebbs and flows of that faulty device.

I once imaginatively traveled to Las Vegas to see an old friend, an old crush, and looked on at her, noticing the uncharacteristically bright, yellow shirt that did not compliment her blond hair and blue eyes at all. Shortly after I returned my imagination to my body and all of my surroundings, my telephone rang. It was my old friend calling to say that she could feel my presence, and she demanded to know that I was alright, imagining that she had intuited some horrendous fate befalling me. I told her that I was fine, and asked what she was wearing, trying hard not to sound like a horny teenager giving a stupid line. She laughed and said that she was wearing some blue jeans that she had drawn all over, as was the style with my group of friends then, and a new yellow shirt that her mom had given her.

The verification of my possible success in "astral projection" disturbed me more deeply than my perceived failure ever had. At least when I thought I was failing, it all made sense. I still felt like I hadn't gone anywhere, that my consciousness had not traveled any further than the throbbing surface of my brain – but at the same time I was being presented with *evidence* of success in viewing events two hundred miles away.

Like a gambler having lost thousands of dollars at the tables, that single hundred-dollar payout spurred my tenacity for the remaining years that it would take for me to experience *real* success in non-local consciousness.

I had taken a job as an apprentice faux finisher under the tutelage of one of the very few Master Faux Painters within hundreds of miles. My mentor happened to be at the same time very sensitive to the spiritual currents around him, and allowed me every opportunity to stretch my non-physical muscles, encouraging my studies into obscure eastern religions and mystical disciplines.

One particular job that we had taken was in a four-story home set on a mesa that overlooked the whole valley. The streets and cars and trees seemed like a town model, a plastic set rather than a part of the world that I lived in.

Before beginning our work every morning, just as the sun was rising over the valley, I would retreat to the highest balcony overlooking the city with a Styrofoam cup of flavored coffee and a morning cigarette, and would allow my mind to sink deep into myself, dropping through rings of reality, from my sleepy Alpha brainwaves into a high to mid-range Theta state, allowing my body to slump just a bit and my focus to remove again from the physical world just a bit before having to jump into the alertness needed to execute the distinctive faux finishes for the day.

Standing one morning on the third floor balcony of the house, I brought my mind into silence, brought my heart into peace, and with all of my awareness I reached out into the space surrounding me and sank deep into *that*, into the space itself.

Everything fell silent as if a wave of frost has frozen the air and the birds and the insects, as if it had seized the engines in the passing cars below and would not allow even a single unholy sound to travel to my ears. In absolute contrast to both the apparent freezing of the world around me as well as the bite of the early morning November cold, my soul was on fire.

I first felt it in my loins, burning like a condensed flame, and then rising up into my stomach like magma, and further to my chest, spreading up my neck and into my head, and down both arms, until my body could no longer contain the heat. It flooded out of my fingers and my toes, from my eyes and from every space between the cells of my skin, running out into the frozen air around me.

My gawking eyes locked onto a specific street below, the details of the intersection barely visible. With one exhaled breath, I was there, having in an instant rushed between the two spaces with an intensity that would have caused me to gasp were I not already exhausting breath at the time of the movement.

I was there, standing on that street, the small, brown house next to me in full detail, the red and yellow leaves littering the sidewalk and spilling into the damp gutters, even the morning frost that barely sheeted the ground. Yet neither the frost nor the leaves crunched under my feet as I moved.

I turned my head to look to the place where I was at just a moment ago, to the large house set above the city, and saw a silver and blue stream of light connecting the balcony of that house to the present street corner. And there was a body standing there, a vacant body that looked quite a bit like me.

No sooner had I looked than I was flung back to that place on the balcony, back towards that vacant body.

My heart slammed as if it had not beaten once since my departure, and my lungs felt as if they were filled with flies. I fell to my knees, coughing and wheezing, finally regaining myself minutes later.

What had just happened? I had moved from one spot to another in an instant, not in my mind, but *I* had actually *moved*. Nothing that I had ever experienced compared to the very concrete and intense projection that I had just achieved. So substantial was the experience that at the time I wasn't able to discern whether my body had taken flight with my enflamed Phoenix soul.

I stood again, quieted my mind and my emotions, still filled with the fanned embers of possibility, and my eyes chose a new target, one father away, another street corner.

Exhaling, I jumped from that balcony to the street, this time consciously slowing my perception of time and space, watching the air and the birds and the cars pass by me, seeing the kinetic ripples caused by my travel moving out away from my body in an unseen energetic spiral, until finally I stood on the other street corner.

A man, obviously not quite ready to greet the day with glee, climbed into his car, cranked the engine on, and pulled out of his driveway only inches away from where I stood, not seeing me at all. I was a conscious and living ghost among the spiritually dead.

I have since referred to this experience of moving my consciousness a short distance away from my body as "jumping," contrasted with "traveling," which implied a greater distance covered as well as an experience in the movement to that remote place.

The term "jumping" was also quite appropriate as the experience itself felt quite a bit like jumping. I could feel the nervousness and excitement building in me just before leaving my body, and the specific type of force of will required seemed much the same as that which as a teen would rise in me nanoseconds before jumping from a rocky cliff into the water below. I had always been terrified of heights, and more so of falling, and had to muster up all of my courage and testosterone and thrill-seeking focus to force my feet to move from the sandstone ridge towards my taunting friends already in the water.

I could not easily define what phobia required a similar daring push to drive my consciousness from my body and my mind, but for quite some time after that first conscious and spontaneous jump, it was indeed a push and a jump that led me from my flesh.

And now I am tasked with quantifying the experience by making it reproducible at will, not for myself, for once I had first jumped from that cliff of solid reality into the ocean of endless possibility, each successive jump required less and less effort. But I must take something for which I had struggled over years to attain and somehow spontaneously was shoved into doing by some supernal part of myself; I have to dissect that thing, and I have to leave you with the pulsating organs.

You cannot use the mind to access the things that are beyond mental comprehension. Forced visualization, image-recall, and all of the other tricks taught by many New Age spiritualists are useless to the aspiring Traveler.

I was working for some time as an occult advisor, tarot reader, and was wiggling my way into spiritual healing. Along with the genuine and consistent clients, I would also see quite a few tourists – people who would pay me for my services all the while denouncing the efficacy of what they were paying me to do. When their past and future were laid out on the table before them, when they would hear their internal and intimate struggles from my mouth, or when their maladies would correct themselves beneath my palms, I would notice a few moments of reverence, followed by a swift and staunch return to cynicism. What was interesting, however, is that *these* clients would often return as well, still scoffing, but nevertheless intent enough on repeating the experience to sacrifice time and money for it.

One such tourist named Travis had heard from a friend that I gave excellent readings into the future. The smiles that Travis and his wife wore when I answered my door made me wonder if they were about to yell, "Trick or Treat!" and present empty pillowcases for me to throw candy into. Travis shook his grin long enough to ask if I was the tarot reader that he had heard about. I invited them both into my living room, lit some scented candles on my coffee table, and asked the couple what had brought them to me.

"Well," Travis hesitated, not quite sure how to approach such an obscure contract, like a teenage boy negotiating his first encounter with a prostitute. "I... we heard that you're pretty good with reading cards and stuff, so we were hoping that you could read cards for us."

I took a deep breath. "This isn't a hobby of mine," I explained. "This is what I do, and this is *who* I am. Not just the tarot, but all of it: spirits, ritual work, divination – all of it. I pay for this home, everything in it, for the car you saw in my driveway, one hundred percent with what I receive from these spiritual workings." I wanted to be clear that I was not a birthday-party-illusionist and that my "tricks" were *not* for entertainment purposes only, despite what the law regarding my profession demanded.

Travis saw that he had offended me. "No, no, we'll pay you, that's not a problem. How much do you charge?"

"That's for you to decide," I told him, which was always my answer to that question. "You can give me whatever you're able to, as you feel is appropriate."

Like most of my first-time clients, my answer made Travis even more uncomfortable. "What do people usually pay you?"

"Some people throw me a twenty-dollar bill, others have given me over a hundred dollars for a reading. It just depends on what you're capable and comfortable with."

Travis nodded his head in apparent understanding and agreement.

"So, are you just looking for a general reading?" I asked. "Just a basic overview of where your life is at and where it might be going?"

"Sure," Travis answered. His wife nodded her head as well.

I shuffled the cards several times before handing them to Travis. "Go ahead and shuffle them however you want, until you're comfortable with them."

By his expression, it was clear that Travis didn't understand the instruction.

"You're basically going to be 'stacking the deck,'" I tried to explain. "Your mind, your superconsciousness, your psychic self, whatever you want to call that part of you that knows everything, will put the cards exactly where they need to be. So, all that you need to consciously do is shuffle the cards and let your intuition tell you when to stop."

He took the cards and tentatively shuffled them, his eyes glancing at me, in hopes of discerning some sort of approval in my expression. His hands started to move the cards between them faster and faster, his eyes shimmering like a mathematician about to crack a lifelong formula.

He stopped. His hands trembling almost unnoticeably, Travis handed the cards back to me. "They're ready," he said, a certain look of trauma on his face, a knowledge that his mind, his hands, all of his lower, physical self had been used for a purpose unknown to his conscious mind.

I laid the cards down and began to read his past, present, and future. While I can't remember a single thing that I said to Travis, I do remember quite clearly his reaction, his hand covering his mouth as it dropped open, his chest rising and falling more quickly than before as he tried to balance his awe by taking in more oxygen, and then finally his body slumping back into the couch, giving up any resistance to the impossible.

Travis and his wife left my home in silence, barely finding the clarity to mumble a thank you as I showed them to the door. I sometimes felt guilty for shattering strangers' sense of reality with the most basic esoteric practices such as divination, and assuaged that emotion with the reminder that *they* had knocked on *my* door, not the other way around.

No more than two weeks passed before I found Travis and his wife knocking again. With a smile, I invited them into my home.

Before I could ask how I could help them, Travis took that initiative.

"Look," he started, "I've been to a lot of 'psychics' and tarot readers and stuff, and they're fun to listen to. But you... you're something else. I mean, man, you just laid out my whole life in front of me and didn't hold back. You're the real McCoy."

"Well, thank you," I smiled and nodded, accepting his compliment. Two or three thick seconds of silence followed, waiting for Travis to come to his point. I forfeited and asked what I could do for him. The question tore the hinges from whatever door was keeping him politely reserved, a storm of words flying from his mouth faster than he could arrange them.

Since he was a child, Travis had imagined that he could travel outside of his body. He had dreamt of taking flight from his flesh into the air above him, floating at his ceiling and looking down on his sleeping body. He fantasized about being able to penetrate walls and thousands of miles of space in a single thought, but as time ticked by, he gave up his dream minute by minute. When he sat on my couch, however, and watched me read into the most private parts of his life, he swore that he recognized in me something special, something of a teacher, a guide who could help him fulfill his most cherished dream.

I had taught a few occult initiates how to project their consciousness outside of their bodies, but never such an objective subject – never a complete neophyte. I would always begin my students with basic meditative practices, bringing the brainwave states into low Theta and holding them there long enough to fall through rings of reality into the superhuman Gamma bursts of realization. Only when this whole gumbo of biochemistry and brainwave states and personal energetic displacement was balanced and solidified would I begin to guide the student into the actual process of leaving the body.

Travis' dream could not wait that long, however. He wanted to fly, and he wanted to fly that very night! And he was asking *me* to provide him with the wings and the silver harness that would allow him to. It was the perfect experiment that I simply could not refuse.

I lowered the lights and asked Travis to remove any jewelry from his body and to sit comfortably with arms uncrossed at his sides. When the ordinary wiggles and adjustments had subsided, I began.

I have always found the task of moving a person into an altered state of consciousness and being much easier and more natural when I, myself, enter that state with them. I am then not just giving commands to my subject, but am going on a journey with a fellow traveler. My words then become both a guide and a narrative.

"Breathe in and feel your chest rising," I said, doing the same. "Breathe out and feel it falling. In and out, up and down. Don't try to make your breath any slower or faster than your body wants it to be; just pay attention to it. The movement of your whole body as you breathe in and out, in and out, is so relaxing.

"You notice a soft light above you, like a cloud of light. You don't have to look at it or see it, just be aware that it's there, and that it is warm and comfortable. And the cloud moves down, down, until it touches the top of your head, and your head relaxes. The cloud moves down, down, touching your ears and your ears relax."

I continued this standard initial relaxation process, guiding both Travis and myself through the relaxation of every limb and muscle until the imaginary cloud was resting beneath our feet and our bodies were both slumped in our chairs, all of my willpower transferred to the operation of my vocal faculties.

We both lingered in low theta brainwaves, our minds threatening to flee into the blackness of delta sleep. I had to tune our brainwaves to approximately 4.5 Hertz, focused upon the goal so that we could peak upwards of 100 Hertz, into the mysterious High Gamma range where miracles are made.

"With your mind – only with your mind – see the room that you're sitting in. Try not to use your body, your senses, or even your brain. The room just comes to life in your vision, like you are waking up from a long sleep."

"I can see it," Travis slurred.

"Great. Now, can you think about your own living room, in *your* house?"

Travis moved his head up and down, signaling in the affirmative.

"Your inner eyes are heavy. Go ahead and close them. Close out the vision of this room. Think about your house, and open your inner vision again. You're waking up again in your own living room."

"Oh wow," Travis interrupted my instruction, his voice animated despite his seeming catatonic composition. "I'm there. Wow."

From that point, Travis was able to move around his house, and then his yard, his neighborhood, and returned to his body a half an hour later. In actuality, all that I had done was guided him down into the Theta state and gave him the direction needed to hold that state long enough to trigger a Gamma reaction.

"I was there, but it was like I wasn't really in control," he reported after he had shook the experience from his joints. "It was like I was watching it instead of really doing, like it wasn't really real, not real like this is real. Like a mix of memory and imagination."

Travis' experience is so un-unique, and is the common starting point in learning to travel outside of the body. Despite the expectedness of the thing, however, it nevertheless seared my ego, and still does, that I could not, in one session, guide him into producing the same sort of out-of-body experience that had reeled me that October morning on the balcony.

I had struggled with the same frustration for over three years, seeming to project my imagination rather than project my *self* to any particular location. Small evidences of success would interrupt my continual doubt and dissatisfaction: people reporting having sensed my presence at the exact moment that I imagined I was with them; being able to accurately describe places I had not previously visited or clothing articles that I had not seen. After a day or two of feeling quite proud of myself, however, the discontent would return, time and again… until that October day when I first learned how not to travel, but to *jump*.

What had brought me to that vital divide between seeing or knowing a thing, and becoming it? What had triggered the final push into spiritual critical mass? How can such an impossibility be quantified?

In my frustration and my assumption that I was getting the whole thing wrong somehow, I tucked my pride deep into my pocket and went to the bookstore to purchase instructional books on astral projection and soul travel. Nearly all of the texts that included the words, "For Beginners" in the title were as vague as they could possibly be, obscuring even what one should expect with astral projection as well as the methods that can be used to achieve such states. Those books that were geared towards Soul Travel, a method of the projection of the consciousness which allowed for the transcendence of the consciousness and experience beyond the astral plane into endless higher and deeper states of being, all verified that I was on the right track – that the initial stages of learning to Soul Travel are indeed imaginative, and that at a certain breaking point, the experience suddenly becomes real.

There are few terms that are more destructive to the recognition of the reality of the esoteric than the word, "Imaginative." This leads to the assumption that all that is done in the arts of Ascent occurs in one's own mind, and goes no further.

In his treatise <u>The Yoga of Power</u>, Julius Evola discusses the value of the imagination in spiritual realization:

> *"This is the power of imagination, understood as the power to see with the mind's eye any given form, in all its details, neatly, and not less clearly than through physical sight...This faculty is to be nourished with an action similar to that exercised by a lens focusing the sun's rays on a spot, in which at the end, a flame is lit. At this level, we may speak of a 'living imagination,' or of a 'magical imagination.'"* [1]

The three or more years that I had spent daily trying to leave my body, viewing the world around me and places at a distance, recreating in my inner vision the environment and the people, struggling to make out the conversations and the faces, was all a process of focusing that magnifying lens of spiritual vision and ability upon the parchment of reality, until one early, October morning, the lens was locked into the precise position to focus the light of the sun to such an intensity that a hole was burned in that parchment. And once I had produced a tiny flame, the whole canvas would soon be incinerated, to unveil a reality beneath the reality, worlds within worlds.

Part II
Taking Flight

With a door open into Limitlessness, all boundaries removed and all possibilities possible, the whole adventure of discovery begins anew.

The microcosm is not just a reflection or representation of the macrocosm. The individual is not a prototype of the whole, but he *is* the whole. His every cell is a solar system of suns orbited by planets orbited by moons, all of these bound together in a galaxy, millions of galaxies composing the universe that is his body. The journey within the self is a journey out into the undiscovered reaches of space. And the exploration into the parts of the self beyond the physical senses is in fact a journey beyond the reaches of creation, into the dimensions beyond space where spirit mingles with thought and desire to create form.

Behind the wall of sight and sound live ten thousand kingdoms to be explored, each with ten thousand paths leading both in and out, and the way to travel upon those paths is as diverse as the countless travelers who walk them.

Chapter Four
The First Tier

In referencing the manifold phenomenon of consciously separating the consciousness and spiritual being from the physical body, the majority of would-be travelers only consider the astral plane and the movement of the consciousness to that state of being.

Through my own travels outside of my body, outside of this plane of matter, and into the most arcane parts of my eternal self, a symbolic "map" of spiritual reality was gradually revealed to me. I insist, however, that this map *is* indeed symbolic, as it is clear that the further away from this physical plane you travel, the less concrete and structured everything is, every line blurring until all that is seen is an ocean of light and sound.

Like an atom, a planet, a solar system, a galaxy, and a universe, the layout of the realms of existence can be imagined as a sphere within a sphere within a sphere. A two-dimensional representation of this would appear as concentric circles.

The nucleus or core of existence is the Eternal Source. This cannot be defined, but only experienced. Like a solar orb, the Eternal Source radiates with light; unlike the sun, however, as the light moves further away from the Source, it does not weaken or dissipate, but instead it solidifies. The first manifestation external of the Source is what I referred to earlier in this text as the Formative Plane. While there are several degrees of this solidification, as well as an abyss, it is at the Formative Plane that the first grand division occurs. That which originally manifested as no manifestation at all, as absolute love, light, and power, finally solidifies to the degree of a visible effect, born in color and song and rushing downwards. Before this division, there was no motion, neither inwards nor outwards but the shining of the Source in all directions and in no direction. There was no travel, in the way that we would consider the word "travel." It is at this first grand division, at the formative plane, that the creation actually begins – where existence is born.

The first embodiment here is born, the Creator, a vague semblance of a head, torso, arms and legs, every appendage and strand of ethereal hair sweeping into a sea of color, the energy and unformed power from Above traveling through the Brahmanic figure like a nexus, flowing down into the worlds without, the will to create a thing being given motion and force, to later take on the characteristics of thought, and then design, and then image, and finally materialize as form.

The original Eternal waves break into power on the formative plane, the Creator there acting as a transformer, molding light into power of a specific sort, and then pushing this through several veils into the condensed form and next plane of thought, often called the Mental Plane.

The Mental Plane begins to bear some resemblance to the physical plane in a more perfect form, glistening with the sunlight of the Eternal Source. While thoughtforms exist here and identities assume the shape of bodies, often in forms appealing to the viewer, everything possess an evanescent and somewhat ghostly quality, as if its shape and substance teeters on a wire between the world of form and causality and that of pure existence.

The Second Grand Division exists here, on the Mental Plane, where causality itself is born, the separation of the infinite into finite forms, the realization of the whole through opposites. Even the ghostly palaces and the translucent bodies can only be recognized because of the empty spaces surrounding them, thus creating the illusion of "something" and "nothing."

Still outwards and downwards the sunlight bears on, the pure thoughts melting and mingling with the objects and subjects of those thoughts, connecting those things below which think, and those other things below which are thought about, as well as a third connection to the process of thinking altogether, and the retention of those thoughts, which is memory. Existing all at once, as there is no distinction between that which has occurred and that which will occur, this Causal Plane is the storehouse and often the visual representation of all memory and all thought from all places and times.

As thought condenses and those rays of original light and the waves of original sound move through the power, the thought, and the consequential value of that thought, the movement itself produces a unique transformation of thought-form into energetic-form, imbued with purpose and given sustainable life through the movement itself, creating astral forms, astral currents, and an entire Astral Plane.

The gradual solidification and condensation of the Eternal light and sound becomes synonymous with a gradually increasing causality and dualism. In the Mental and Causal Planes, this dualism is necessary to distinguish between the formed and the unformed, the objects and the spaces between them. In the Astral Plane, however, dualism becomes fanatical, where emotions swell in favor of one thing over another, and nonsensical ideas like "good" and "evil" are born. In the realms above, embodiments carried on specific tasks and served specific functions in their existence. It seems that on the astral plane, however, there is very little method at all. The seemingly divine organization that is so apparent in the Mental Plane is entirely lost on the Astral, in a jumble of kingdoms and gateways, gods, devils, spirits, angels, elemental personifications, all scurrying to and fro for some entirely indistinguishable purpose.

The movement of power into thought, thought into form, and form into energy, completes its linear descent in the physical plane, the realm of flesh and substance, where the spiritual organization of things seems lost and duality is no longer an abstract, but is a concrete and inescapable reality. The creative force, the light and sound of the Eternal Source, here manifests not as spirit, but as flesh, as dust, as rock and water, as planets and electrons.

Through each stage of the densification of power, identity becomes increasingly separate from all things that are seen as being external from the self. At the physical plane, rocks no longer recognize their godhood, nor do plants, minerals, or most animals. Identity becomes attached to form. Dirt thinks that it is dirt, flowers think that they are flowers, and humans think that they are simply humans. It then becomes the task of the individual to remember, to pierce with their awareness beyond the form into their True Identity.

These planes are not separated from one another with walls, however, but with curtains of shadow, easily penetrated, often even by accident, by entities, objects, energies, and projections of every sort from either side of the curtain. Conscious of our own potential, hopeful for our own godhood, although even the comprehension of such a state is impossible for the human brain, we are able to formulate methods by which we can pierce the shadow walls and ride the tide back to the Eternal Source.

It seems that a downwards or outwards flow – moving from a less concrete realm and form into that of a more concrete realm and form - is more common and requires less effort than the reverse. Moving from this outermost realm of the flesh into the worlds of spirit sets the Traveler against a current of energetic movement. Conscious will, direct intention, and perseverance against the raging accusations of the intellect are required not to leave the body, but to Travel away from it entirely.

The last century has been an era of remarkable change in the world in every imaginable manner, not least of which includes the awakening of the human psyche, on a near worldwide scale, to the hidden and powerful aspects of the individual. With the rising interest in hermeticism, theosophy, the occult, and even psychedelics, the subject of "Astral Projection" has been a hum and a buzz throughout the spiritual community. From books on astral projection to urban legends of the subject, to séance circles and ouija boards, contact with astral entities, projection of the consciousness into the astral plane, and the opening of astral gateways has remained throughout this worldwide awakening a diamond in a coal mine.

Recalling the description above of the descendant grades of spiritual evolution from unformed power towards a gradual densification of intention, it is clear that the astral realm is only a short step away from the physical plane. Astral forms, intelligences, and entities slide to our side of the veil on a daily, if not hourly basis. Some of these entities are worshipped by physical inhabitants as "gods," most world religions turning their attention not towards the Eternal Source of all things as their devotional focus, but a creation of that Power, and a creation that is quite nearer to the simple and flawed physical state than to the perfect and incomprehensible God State.

Gateways into that astral world surround us in the forms of spiritual symbols, occult devices, spoken words, ancient temples, and even certain types of metal or wood. The shadows that separate the physical plane from the astral plane have worn thin in some places, where travel has occurred in either direction enough times to carve a natural pathway between the two.

As unimpressive as the astral plane may be to the seasoned Traveler, however, it is inarguably the first step on the rung of Ascent. No other planes can be reached without first dirtying the soles of the feet in the astral clutter that awaits.

Methods of Projection

Imagining myself becoming a rose didn't do the trick to get me out of my body, but I cannot blame the failure on the method alone, as my own spiritual incontinence and lack of psychic balance could just as easily have been the culprit. In fact, I could look back at dozens of methods that I used in my attempts to astral project, and I could call them all failures, not counting them as stepping stones to an eventual and lasting success.

A good deal of the written and passed-along guidance on achieving an out-of-body-experience approaches the whole matter with a sidestep – with games to trick the mind into watching the right hand while the left hand pulls the spirit out of the hat. All of these tricks confused rather than enlightened or empowered me towards the goal. Such games are very easy to point to when looking for something to blame my years of failure on.

If the object is to leave your body, then you should leave your body. If the task were to become a rose, or to find the door to December[1], we would be dealing with a different matter.

The same method that I used to guide Travis out of his body and into his distant house can be applied without a guide, through a type of self induced trance. I hesitate to refer to this trance as "self-hypnosis," in large due to the confusion and hype over what hypnosis exactly is. Most people live their lives, minute-to-minute, in some degree of hypnosis: while working at a job that dictates thought patterns; driving down the road, unconscious competence or incompetence dictating speed and stops and movements and turns, lights and signs of certain colors with pre-programmed meanings demanding certain actions; while relaxing in front of the television, being bombarded by political or religious propaganda, commercial advertisements, and a concocted sense of relatedness to the characters in the film; even while spending time with family, completing the tasks of the chore lists and the preparations for an outing, the time spent on certain activities, attention yanked here and there to create an equal sharing of yourself. We all live our lives in a programmed and hypnotic state; no swinging pocket watches are required.

Now, we can become our own programmers and our own hypnotists.

Lower the lights, remove jewelry and any restrictive clothing, and take a seat in a comfortable chair. It also might help to ensure the temperature is constant and comfortable. Seventy-four degrees Fahrenheit is usually cool enough to keep the skin from itching and to keep the sweat glands normal, while still being warm enough to avoid shivering.

Let yourself wiggle in the chair for a few moments. Move your wrists and your ankles, wiggle your fingers and toes, move your head about loosely. If you don't get these wiggles out from the start, you most certainly will twitch and adjust once you have begun.

Breathe in and feel your chest rising. Breathe out and feel it falling. In and out, up and down. Don't try to make your breath any slower or faster than your body wants it to be; just pay attention to it. The movement of your whole body as you breathe in and out, in and out, is relaxing.

Notice a soft light above you, like a cloud of light. You don't have to look at it or see it, just be aware that it's there, and that it is warm and comfortable. And the cloud moves down, down, until it touches the top of your head, and your head relaxes. The cloud moves down, down, touching your ears and your ears relax.

Continue this initial relaxation process, guiding yourself through the relaxation of every limb and muscle until the imaginary cloud rests beneath your feet and your body is slumped in your chair.

You will then be very close to Theta brainwaves, if not exactly there. The brain is in a Beta state when high levels of concentration are reached and held, like when studying or problem-solving. Lower than Beta is Alpha, when the mind is not functioning on one particular goal, but is on "auto-pilot," watching television, reading an entertaining novel, washing dishes, and going about daily life. The first steps of lowering the lights and wiggling the body took the brain from Beta, from thinking, "I have to do this right. I'm going to be Soul Traveling in a few minutes! I can't screw this up. What did he say was the first step?" to Alpha, "Okay, one step at a time, I'll just breathe for right now." Delta is the point when you fall asleep, or in any other way lose consciousness. Theta is that in-between state, in-between awake and asleep, in between here and there, in between this world and the other. It is the door that once is cracked can allow the Soul to sneak out of the body, out of this realm, past the parent's bedroom and into the wondrous night sky.

The brainwaves then have to be tuned to approximately 4.5 Hertz, focused upon the goal so that you can peak upwards of 100 Hertz, into the mysterious High Gamma range where miracles are made. Only through that door of Theta can the highest Gamma brainwave states be sustained, lest they crash like sudden waves on the beach before breaking into a crest.

With your mind – only with your mind – see the room that you're sitting in. Try not to use your body, your senses, or even your brain. The room just comes to life in your vision, like you are waking up from a long sleep.

Imagine yourself standing up out of your chair. Don't think about it, don't ask yourself how you would move if you were a spirit, don't dissect the whole thing with your intellect. Simply stand up from your chair.

Two keys can be used here. The first is to move forwards and outwards with an exhalation of your breath. This facilitates a movement away from yourself, as if your Soul is carried on the current of air leaving your body, away from your body. Another key is to keep the experience and your visualization of it *in first person*. It is far too easy here, especially in such a fragile state as Theta, to allow imagination to take the place of visualization. They are two distinct and separate functions of consciousness. The visualization that you must employ is that very same *living imagination* that was spoken of earlier. The fantasy-imagination is easy to spot, as your room will no longer look like your room, and the objects in it, even the walls themselves, will be replaced by entertaining and cartoonish representations of your room. And your vision through your eyes will be replaced by your vision from outside of yourself. Note that at this point, "yourself" no longer refers to your body, your brain, or anything dealing with the meaty mechanism lumped on the chair, but is instead that undying self that stands up and moves about the room without the aid of a physical device.

Move about as you wish. You can even travel, in the twinkling of an eye, to any place in the world. You can observe friends, lovers, enemies, family, world leaders, and rock stars.

This process, at first, is more of a mental or imaginative projection than any sort of astral or spiritual travel. This is the beginning of a sort of "bi-location," your brain still in your body but your mind in another place, no longer local to your brain, but still delivering the mind's messages to its previous host.

The temptation to dismiss this whole experience as a fraudulent creation of a childish imagination is very tempting, especially for those who lack the self-discipline to see this to the end. Follow this path, however, and no door will ever shut you out again.

Continued daily practice of mental projection will lead to not only a clearer view of that which is observed, but also a more accurate telling of the events which you are observing.

There is no definite line between mental travel and Soul Travel, but once you have crossed from one to the other, you will be very sure of it. Your desire to substantiate your visions will cease, your struggle to accept that which you see will fall away, and you will be left with the realization that what you have sought after was yours all along.

Performing a substantial "jump" from one place to another will be easy. Pick a spot that you can barely see off in the distance, and go there with a single breath.

You are thus prepared to enter the manifold gates of magic and miracle.

At the Gates

At sixteen years old I had been dabbling in the occult for about a year, and had experienced enough success to recognize the efficacy of my ritual workings. My attempts at evocation had been more successful than my work on astral projection; I had called into this world several different astral entities, and although I could not see them at that time, their presence was nonetheless obvious.

Aside from a couple of friends that would join me on the weekends for ouija board sessions, candle magick spells, and eventually group evocations, I found myself quite alone at school. As my obsession with the occult grew, and the effects of such were increasingly more evident in my appearance and behavior, I began to create a magnetic push and pull with those around me, drawing them into my secret world, but at the same time repelling them from me altogether. Dustin and Lee had classes off-campus, taking a courses in welding and other trades from the college for which they received both college and high school credits, and so I found myself eating lunch alone every day, which was a celebration rather than a disturbance for me, as I was able to get away from the noise and the jostling of my "peers."

Searching for a boiler room, which seemed to appear in every movie and television show set in high school but which seemed to be entirely absent in any that I had attended, I instead found a hallway near the gym locker rooms that was deserted during lunch hour. I would sit on steps that led down to the football field, eat my lunch, read my latest New Age book, and would end my break with a cigarette before returning to class.

As I sat alone, I heard short but heavy footsteps approaching. I shoved my books, cigarettes, and food back into my bag and acted as if I was tying my shoes. Teachers and other adults in my life had always shown concern for me. Rather than playing with kids at recess in elementary school, I instead chose to sit inside and draw or fold paper into amazing creatures. Rather than running with the other boys at church campouts, I would sit around the fire with the adults, listening to their conversations and trying to join in when I could. Not only did I seem to make those my age uncomfortable with my realization that we had very little in common, but I also made adults even more uncomfortable.

"Go play with the other kids," "go hang out with your friends," and "go be with other people" were phrases that I heard again and again through my life. I didn't like other people, I didn't enjoy playing with other kids, and goddamnit I really didn't have any friends. And so I waited to hear these things again from whoever was approaching my once-hidden lunch spot.

"I didn't know anybody else knew about this place," a girl's voice scuffled out instead. I looked at my would-be accuser to find a girl that I had seen around school and who was in a few of a my classes, Lynette, a midget, a loner, and most disturbing to me, a hippie. She wore flowered dresses that covered her ankles, Birkenstock sandals, hemp necklaces, and straight, uneventful hair. I had never tried to talk to her before... I was never interested. She was just another person, and I did not like people. Nevertheless, she sat next to me, drew out her own sandwich, and joined me for lunch.

After plenty of silence, which did not seem uncomfortable in the least to her, she asked, "So, you're into witchcraft and stuff?" as she finished her sandwich, with the same nonchalance as asking about a homework assignment.

"Yeah, I guess."

"Cool. Me too. I worship Diana."

"Cool." I had no idea who Diana was, but I wasn't about to set myself up for another opportunity to prove my ignorance.

"You should come over to my sister's house tonight," Lynette invited, as if we had been friends for years. "We get together with a bunch of people every Friday, call the Watchtowers, invoke the elements, all of that."

My annoyance was transfigured into sincere interest. The fact that there was one other occultist in my school was enough to perk my attention, but to imagine a house filled with them was irresistible.

I met with Lynette after school and walked a few miles to her sister's house. Aside from having to cut my stride in half to accommodate her small body, her company was enjoyable. Nothing seemed to shock or disturb her, nothing seemed to shake her. She existed in a world that was her own, and it was absolutely impenetrable.

After lounging around the front yard of Lynette's sister Suzie's house for a couple of hours, cars started appearing and dropping off people, some who I knew from school and others whom I had never seen before. Led Zeppelin's song, "Stairway to Heaven" had just started playing when Suzie finally arrived. It was the first time I'd ever heard it. Jimmy Page's opening guitar strums and Robert Plant's humming voice were filled with magic. That song became our hymn as we congregated in our small group. Suzie and Lynette hugged and in the same motion as they slid away from each other their hands glided along the arms of the other until only their fingers were touching. With mutual smiles, they began to walk in a circle, beginning a slow dance, weaving in and out of the other's arms, never releasing their hands but seeming not the least bit restricted in their motion nonetheless.

I lit a cigarette and watched, entranced, feeling as if I had found myself in the midst of an ancient Celtic celebration. My family hugged as rich and as deep as these sisters had about as rarely as we gazed into each other's eyes with the profound and obvious love and respect that they held for each other. Dancing with one another, in my family, would be unheard of unless it could be done in laughter and jest.

A tall, thin guy wearing a torn up Misfits shirt and a Glenn Danzig haircut sat next to me and asked for a cigarette. I handed him a cigarette, which he took a few good minutes to light to his satisfaction.

"So, I've seen you around school," he said, his words carried into the air on a thick cloud of cigarette smoke. "You're into witchcraft and stuff, right?" This seemed to be the only detail about me that anyone recognized. I knew that I wasn't trying to hide my interest and involvement in the occult, but at the same time I hadn't yet begun to advertise it, or so I thought.

"Yeah," I answered, sticking to the philosophy of 'less-is-more.'

"Have you ever heard of the Necronomicon?"

The book that he was referring to is a grimoire written and compiled in the late 1970's, claiming to be an ancient and fabled book of magick taken from ancient Sumeria. Although the grimoire is an obvious fake, inasmuch as the backstory and history is concerned, its efficacy as a ritual tool has remained quite notorious since its first release. Aside from rituals of evocations, spells of bane and benevolence, and exorcisms, the Necronomicon includes a lengthy section on opening and entering astral gates to each of the planetary spheres, through which the Magician can travel and eventually meet with the gods of each sphere, accumulating immense occult power and superhuman faculties as he travels from one to the next.

"Yeah, I've worked out of it," I answered.

"Have you 'Walked the Gates'?" Cory asked.

"No, no," I said. "I haven't gotten that far, yet. I'm still working with the Watchers and such. But I'm planning on entering the Gates soon."

"It's intense," he said. "It's not like anything you've ever experienced before."

After the song had played a good two or three times, the group of about ten of us went inside. Suzie stood and announced that we were going to call the Watchtowers. I had done this several times before on my own, and I wanted to thrust my hand in the air as if in school to nominate myself to be among the four chosen to give the call of a particular cardinal direction and element, but was sure that such was not acceptable in this setting. Suzie called on three others, aside from herself, to give the calls. We stood in a circle, the four chosen standing in the approximate location of their particular cardinal point, and joined hands. Suzie, standing in the east, began, raising her hands into the air, causing the circle of us to do the same.

"I call thee, Guardians of the Watchtowers of the East, spirits of air, to come to this Circle to protect and empower it." The group was silent, their concentration tangible, their focused will and energy pulling the invoked forces to us.

The next person began, "I call thee, Guardians of the Watchtowers of the South, spirits of fire, to come to this Circle to protect and empower it." The same silence followed, but the presence that had been drawn into the room with the previous call multiplied. My arms trembled and I was forced to turn my attention away from the ritual and towards my breathing, as I could feel my entire torso compressing as if being wrapped by an invisible boa.

"I call thee, Guardians of the Watchtowers of the West, spirits of water, to come to this Circle to protect and empower it." I wasn't ready for the call to come so fast, and brought my mind back to the Circle, back to the ritual.

"I call thee, Guardians of the Watchtowers of the North, spirits of earth, to come to this Circle to protect and empower it."

As our silent pulling upon the energies of the elements waned and I began to wonder what we would do with the power that steamed from the group of us, the chain of hands broke along with the silence, people were again chatting, and soon music was again blaring. And I stood in the center of the room, unmoved from my spot, shaken by the power of collective will yet troubled by the apparent disrespect of the forces invoked by returning to such activities after an obvious encounter with the spiritual. Once my contempt had passed, however, I returned to a seat on the floor, still aware of the supernal presence in the room, but content to enjoy the night and to take from it my own lessons.

I hadn't noticed Cory before our meeting at Suzie's, but the following school-day, I saw him in the halls between each class, as if my awareness of his existence solidified his presence somehow. Foregoing my usual, solitary lunch break, I found him sitting on the floor, back against his locker, eating, and asked if I could join him. Our conversation about the gates of the <u>Necronomicon</u> was far from finished.

"So, what is it like," I asked, "to enter the Gates?"

"Have you ever tried acid?" he asked.

"Ummm... no."

"Well, it's kind of like that, without the acid." I raised an eyebrow. "It's like, you draw the gate on the ground, light the lanterns in the corners, you give the conjuration of the Gate, and then you lay on the ground, and you see the gate appear in the sky. It just... appears there!"

"You actually saw it, with your eyes?" I asked, not sure if I'd believe his answer anyways.

"Look," he asserted, annoyance stretching the word, "It's not like I just imagined the whole thing. The fucking gate appeared in the sky, right in front of me."

"So, did you go into it?"

Cory paused, a long pause almost hinting of shame or embarrassment. "I don't remember."

"What do you mean, you don't remember?" I couldn't believe this! How could you open an astral gate, see it in full detail in front of you, but not remember if you went inside of it or not?

"I blacked out," Cory admitted. "I don't know what happened. I saw the gate right there, it started to open, and the next thing I knew I was laying on the grass and the sun was up. I blacked out, and was out until the morning."

"So, could the whole thing have just been a dream?" I prodded, not wanting to discard his entire experience, but still needing to know.

"I told you, I didn't imagine it." Cory stood up and walked away.

Whether Cory's experience was indeed a dream, or if it had actually happened was irrelevant. All that mattered is that I knew that such a thing was possible, to find or to manufacture a gateway leading into the other world, and that if the mind can be kept from falling into Delta sleep, I could pass into that other world.

On the night of the full moon, I replaced the textbooks, three-ring binders, and notebook paper in my backpack with a ritual dagger, four oil lamps, a bottle of lamp oil, a bowl with the inscriptions of the Watcher drawn thereon, a few rounds of charcoal, and a small bag of incense resin.

Years previous, when I was ten, my mother and her then husband, James, bought a large house in a barely-developed rural area just outside of town that sat at the base of a small mountain that hosted several caves. My step-brother and I had roamed the desert together, usually with .22 rifles or shotguns in hand, searching for jackrabbits, beer bottles, discarded household appliances, or even coyotes to shoot. In our excursions, we would often take refuge from the 110 degree summer heat inside of these caves, eating lunch there before continuing on our hunt. One cave in particular somehow "felt" more alive and more welcoming than any other. It was to this cave that I would retreat to perform some of my first rituals, calling out to the elements or to the spirits or demons or whatever forces I was intent on calling, and in that cave, they would rise.

And to that cave I hiked, with only the moonlight guiding me, my bulging pack rustling on my back while I negotiated boulders as stepping stones over a slide of red dirt that would otherwise deliver me again to the bottom of the mountain.

After catching my breath, I unpacked my bag, and with my black-handled dagger, I scrawled the image of the first gate, the Gate of Nanna, the horned God of the Moon, in the compacted sandstone floor.

I filled the thirsty lanterns with their oil, placed them in their cardinal positions, and lit their wicks, the whole cavern bursting into a glow. I called out to the Watcher, as I had done many times before. And as always, I could feel Them rushing into the cave from above and from below, and lurking outside of the inscribed gate. I lit the coal in the bowl and dumped my bag of incense on them. Standing in the north with the Necronomicon in my hands, my eyes strained to make out the small words on the shadowed pages, and I began to walk to the east, and then the south, to the west, and back to the north, reading aloud the incantation of the gate.

"Spirit of the moon, remember. Nanna, father of the astral gods, remember."

The grimoire called for thirty clockwise revolutions around the gate, but the task of making out the words of the incantation and estimating the meter of the cadence was a pull on my mental faculties as it was, and so I continued the incantation as best I could, trying to keep my feet from moving too fast or too slow.

The circumambulations, the incantation, the incense, and the energy that began to pulse through the gateway started to overwhelm my physical being halfway through the speaking of the incantation. My head started to spin, my words started to slur, and as I struggled with the pronunciation of the barbarous words, I could tell that I was going to go down at any moment. I stopped at the north, no longer able to walk, and finished the last line of the incantation. No sooner was it spoken did I fall to the ground, not unconscious, but not in this world either. I was somewhere in between, my mind being sucked into some unseen vortex above me.

As if I was dreaming with my eyes open, an image formed in the sky, lines being scrawled in the moonlight and stars like a hallucination that I couldn't blink away. My breath was sucked towards that gate with the same force that pulled my gaze. I could feel my eyelids closing, and I tried in vain to fight them, every muscle in my face tightening to avoid the inevitable sleep that was pressing down on me.

Just as quickly as I had gone down, I then went out. My eyes closed, and I could feel my mind dropping, but not into a usual sleep, not into a sleep at all, but into a conscious dream in which I was walking in a city above the clouds, the horizon filled with stars and the landscape sprinkled with shimmering palaces.

My eyes opened again after what seemed like hours in that other place. I climbed to my feet, a bit embarrassed, wondering if what I had experienced was the ritual's success, or its absolute failure. The lines in the dirt floor and the burnt out lantern wicks seemed like relics from a distant past. I shoved all of the ritual items in my backpack, confused and somewhat angry, and hurried home to catch some real sleep before morning.

Over the next month, I could only conclude that what I had experienced was indeed the success of the Working – that I had actually walked through the astral gate into another world, although remaining completely conscious and lucid throughout the travel didn't seem possible. Continuing on to the gate of Mercury, then to Venus, and on and on until I had entered the gate of Saturn, I retained my consciousness more and more with each Walking, and my mind retained more and more details of the kingdom to which I had traveled.

The month of waiting between each ritual of entering the astral gate was not spent solely on the <u>Necronomicon</u> and its powers. Nor did my journey through dimensional portals end once the final gate had been entered.

I was in high school, only seventeen years old, and a reputation began to lurk ahead of me as I went. While the talk of my dealings with spirits and my black rituals mortified my party-going older sister and my sophomore-class-president younger sister, it opened quite a few people into conversations that they would otherwise not have had. As these casual encounters turned into requests, and even paid contracts, for spiritual assistance, opportunities to explore other gateways into the spiritual realms presented themselves.

Layne was a tall, red-headed kid that just about everyone knew in our school. It would be difficult to refer to him as a classmate, as no one can recall ever seeing him in class. He could always be found before school, at lunch breaks, and after school by looking a few feet above eye-level for a cloud of thick, white smoke. Layne was a proud distributor, retailer, and personal user of marijuana, a fact that he never tried to hide from family, friends, or authorities. At some point between seventeen and eighteen years old, he had become legally emancipated and shared a two-story house with a couple of friends.

As uncensored about everything as he was about pot, Layne asked me while hanging out in the parking lot with quite a group of people if the rumors about me conjuring up demons and spirits were true. When I confirmed the suspicions, he asked that, since I was able to call them *into* this world, if I could make them *leave* this world as well. I told him that most entities can be guided into leaving this realm once they are here, and that very few put up any sort of resistance when they are urged to do so. Layne explained that his house was haunted by some sort of phantom. He and his roommates had just put up with the doors slamming shut on their own and the lights being switched off and on without assistance from a hand, but that recently the activity had intensified, guests being grabbed by invisible hands and one girl feeling as if she was being suffocated while she slept.

I wrote down his address and set a date and time to "check out" his house.

I arrived to Layne's house prepared. My backpack, which was increasingly used more for ritual items than school books, was again bulging, this time with a silver chalice; a couple quarts of saltwater, prepared beforehand for the purpose of exorcism; and a black, hooded robe that I insisted on donning at any excuse, despite the insistence of all of my friends that the thing was ridiculous and drew away from any ability to focus on the spiritual task at hand.

Layne answered the door and invited me in. His house was a bit fuller than I had imagined it would be, girls chatting in the kitchen over drinks, a few people playing a video game in front of the television, and general traffic through every bedroom in the house. As if I was simply another party-guest, Layne plopped down on his sofa and grabbed a game remote from one of his friends.

"So, where's this thing I'm looking for?" I reminded him, trying to covertly ask about the entity, as to avoid embarrassing him.

"Oh, the demon-ghost-thingy," he replied, as if he had just remembered why I was there. "Yeah, if you go down the hall there you'll see some stairs, and that's where I think it hangs out the most."

His eyes didn't move from the television screen once.

"Does it *only* stay down there?" I asked.

"No, no..." he paused to execute some special combination move on his game before returning a quarter of his attention to our conversation. "It's basically all over the house, in every room. Just, everywhere."

I looked around at the minimum of a dozen people. "Okay, dude, if you want me to get rid of this thing, I'm going to need to go in all of your rooms and..."

"Yeah," he interrupted, no longer able to devote *any* attention to the matter at hand. "Just do whatever you need to do. It's no problem."

I spent a few long seconds deciding whether to return through the front door or to stay and help my friend. It is possible that my obsessive interest in the paranormal, however, took precedence over either impetus and forced me down the hallway towards the stairs.

The warm, summer air drew cold and stale the closer I got to the basement. I could *feel* the spirits down there. Spirits. Plural. Perhaps a legion of them. As I descended the wooden steps with creaks and crackles, the spirits became aware of me, aware of my presence, my intrusion. They moved from their widdershins dance in the center of the basement to the steps, spinning around me instead, dancing around me like witches at a Sabbat.

I fumbled around in my bag, retrieving the bottle of consecrated water. I dumped it in the silver chalice, my gaze not moving from the living shadows around me, afraid that the moment I looked away they would dive into the center of their spiritual whirlpool and devour me.

Dipping my index and middle finger into the water, I retrieved it with a flick and cast burning droplets of cool saltwater on the floor. With muted shrieks the throng of spirits dissipated. Again and again, the water fell to the floor, my lips reciting some special exorcism that now eludes the grip of my memory. In the same moment that the basement was completely clear of all ghostly presence, the same moment that the goose bumps on my skin flattened and the air seemed breathable once more, the relief was torn away by the reemergence of the spirits in one specific corner of the basement. I flung drops of water, more violently now, as if I could damage their incorporeal bodies with the momentum of the droplets. The spirits again vanished, and just as quickly rose again in that same corner, as if an invisible curtain hung in that space with a slit in the fabric large enough to allow the passage of these entities from the backstage of the astral realm to the center stage of this world.

I set the chalice on the floor, recognizing that I was staring into an opening between the worlds, a spot that had been rubbed thin enough to provide an overlapping of the spiritual and the physical.

Through various exorcisms, Banishing Rituals, and Closings, the spirits finally ceased their trespass into this world.

I reported this experience to Layne, after sprinkling the rest of the house with the consecrated water. I invited him to contact me if any further activity occurred. He never did.

Through the Wilderness

These planes are not separated from one another with walls, however, but with curtains of shadow, easily penetrated, often even by accident, by entities, objects, energies, and projections of every sort from either side of the curtain.

In our search for conscious contact with the spiritual, we as a self-aware species, have discovered ten thousand ways to displace the shadows between our worlds long enough to pass through to the other side, or to call other things from that other side to pass through to here. The planets, the distant stars, the elements of nature, the signs of the tarot, the symbols of spirits or of spiritual kingdoms, astral gateways drawn on the ground, and countless other devices can be used as bridges from the world of substance to the world of energy.

The astral plane is cluttered with images and activity, so much so that the Traveler must be quite intentional in his travels to the other side. Once he has arrived at the specific region of the astral that he wishes to visit, however, the experiences and knowledge that can be gained seem endless. Every entity, angel, demon, and even the gods can be found there on the astral, and can be communicated with in absolute clarity and conversation.

This astral plane, regardless of its promise, is only the beginning, the first step into endless worlds of power and enlightenment.

Chapter Five
The Second Tier

Beyond the borders of the astral plane, just as the din of a million psychic voices fades, other worlds come into view - quieter, more organized and inviting worlds.

The separation between the causal and the mental planes is tenuous, not divided by shadows but by the vague fog of ancient memory. Memory itself is the great distinction between the two planes: while the mental plane is the realm of present thought and formation, the causal plane is the spiritual and substantial representation of the nexus of consciousness. The causal plane is an experiential construct of all that has, is, and will be conceived, existing not as a linear pattern, as we consider memory to be, but instead as a collage and a pallet of all existing together.

The noises of the astral plane, caused by the struggle to dominate and exert the particular energy, task, and temporal existence of the individual entities, forms, and currents existing on that plane ceases in the causal, where duality begins to fade. "Your" thoughts and "my" thoughts and "theirs" and the others dissolve just as meaninglessly as those concepts of the past and those of the future can merge into the quiet hum of the present.

It is also in the causal realm that we begin to experience not only a transfer of consciousness into another dimension, but also a *transfiguration* of consciousness itself, to allow the integration of the experiences of that plane.

We ordinarily exist not only in the physical state, but also quite strongly in the astral state, in a state of emotions and perceptions and overlaps of the two worlds. Our religions, metaphysics, sciences, arts, and even our interaction with others of our species occur in the physio-astral state. Crossing the bridge between the astral and the higher planes means leaving behind our assumptions of existence, of ourselves, and of the importance of things, and beginning to accept the supreme reality, which is that none of that which we once considered to be fatal, true, or even important is – that we have been living in a cage of our own assumptions.

Every spiritual Master has taught that the ultimate goal of the Chela ought to be nonattachment from all that is not Eternal, and that the path of nonattachment is the middle path which leads towards enlightenment and immortality. The idea of nonattachment itself is a bit of a trap, as some adherents might begin to neglect familial and social responsibilities, friendships, relationships, and every inner tie to their fellow man out of a desire to turn the fullness of their focus onto the Eternal. The trick, or the ruse, is, however, that all things are manifestations of the Eternal Source. Nothing exists that is not It. What is necessary, then, is to rise above the astral state, the state of emotional attachment, of emotional needing and longing and internal suffering of ten thousand forms, into first the causal plane, where all minds and all awareness and all perceptions are one. This is the state often referred to as the Universal Consciousness. It is first in this causal state that you can begin to understand that it is not the actions or behaviors that are of any Eternal importance, but the internal state.

Entering the astral plane is an easy task, once you have discovered a gateway or have managed to slip through a thin spot between the worlds. Leaving it is a different task altogether. There are no gateways between the astral and causal. There are no ov365erlaps or thin spots. The shadows that separate these two planes are thick and bright and loud.

Whereas individuals can easily slip from their physical, waking state into the astral state, travel from the ordinary physical, conscious state to the consciousness of the causal must be quite deliberate. The planes ruling the mental faculties are linked in the individual by the mental processes. Mind and its singular focus is the key and the gateway.

What can be focused upon, however, to enter these new worlds is quite a controversial matter. One does not simply climb the Astral Tree, pop into the Da'ath Sephiroth, and find himself in the majesty of the higher planes. The intention must exist before the flight to enter into the causal plane, and not only into the realm itself, but into a specific region of it for a specific purpose. This, in itself, becomes daunting for the Seeker who simply desires to climb the latter to heaven.

Gurus and Spiritual Masters insist that in order to travel any higher than the astral plane, the Seeker can only do so with the assistance from a guru or Master, creating a sort of monopoly on what would otherwise be an entirely natural and even inevitable Ascent from our state of mortality and the cycle of struggle into the limitless peace and power of our True Identity.

As with all things, there is falsehood wrapped inside of truth, wrapped inside of misunderstandings, with another sprinkle of truth on the candy shell. The truth of the matter of utilizing the assistance of a specific guru or Master to transmigrate the various planes and state of existence is that the image of that Bodhisattva can be held in the mind, the attention turned fully towards him or her, and the Soul Travel that ensues while basking in the presence of that teacher will draw the soul straight through the astral plane into the realm in which that Master resides. Without fail, upon arriving to greet the Master on the Higher Planes, he or she will smile, your presence in their temple not only welcomed but anticipated.

The mental visualization of objects or structures can also be used to transport your consciousness to these realms of consciousness. As you focus your mind on the object as you lower your consciousness through rings of reality, and as you leave your body, you will find yourself awakening not in this world or in the astral, but before that very object. There is a unique planar displacement that occurs when bypassing realms in such a manner, in which it seems that the whole of reality trembles and convulses before giving up its hold on your perception.

The trick here, however, is in the visualization of the object, structure, or embodiment of the causal or astral plane; more appropriately, it is in the acquisition of the initial image of such, as in order to recall such an item, that item must be observed in the first place to be stored in the memory. Luckily for the Traveler, however, the mind is permanently and constantly plugged in to the mental and the causal planes. Anything that has ever been conceived or perceived originates in the mental plane and all of its details are stored in the causal plane.

A degree of inner quietude and of self-trust is needed to access these images for your own use. In meditation, allow your inner vision to collect the visual details of a suitable object from the other side, specifically from the causal or mental plane. Put away your expectations of how such an object might appear, or what it might be, and allow your inner vision to simply receive. It is the nature of the mind to connect to these two planes when turned over to itself, the crutches of the external senses being kicked away.

Having obtained such an image in your mind, focusing in on it while projecting your consciousness outside of your body; once the planar displacement has subsided you will find that you have been transported in the twinkling of an eye before that object and on the causal or the mental plane.

The differentiating factor between these two planes is the linear nature of the events and surroundings within them.

Time and space being Maya dissipate gradually the further away from the concrete and solidified outer realm of reality that we move, bringing our consciousness back to the original Source.

The causal plane will therefore appear quite linear and structured. Conversations with natives of this plane will occur in quite the same manner as they would on earth; paths will lead to destinations; structures will exist as one glowing, azure stone atop another; etc. The mental plane, by contrast, might feature conversations in which the salutation and the valediction occur at once, as well as the body of the communication; the destination will be reached before a foot is laid onto the path; and the bodies and the structures and the objects are no longer layered, as they are so clearly in the physical plane, but all bodies can be interacted with at once.

For this reason, the early Traveler might become easily overwhelmed by visits to the mental plane before the causal plane has been thoroughly explored.

Once the nonlinear mindstate can be withstood for any amount of time, you will find your awareness itself experiencing an immersion into the collective unconscious. This is not yet a dissolution of the self into the Greater Self, which is not a "self" at all, but which is the existence of all things in one field of thought and energy, but it is the beginning. You will experience thought and understanding from the vantage of another, or from no vantage at all, and you will become keenly aware of the lack of any real separation, at least in consciousness, between yourself and anything else that exists.

We've traveled now from the physical to the astral, back to the body, and then bypassed the path of the astral on a psychic overpass to get to the causal. Now, how does one get from the causal to the mental, or from the physical to specifically one of these two realms?

The interconnectedness of these two planes lend favorably to the travels of the Seeker, as all that is necessary once ethereal foot is in that heaven is to *think* the matter, and it will manifest. Thought alone can carry you between these planes, and to any location on them. Distances are only traveled conventionally if the mind holds to the idea that they must be. Otherwise, the shortest distance between two non-existent points is the inversion of the points in relation to your present position.

In fact, once on the mental plane and all of the realms Above, you will begin to notice that you are not traveling much anywhere at all, but that as your consciousness shifts from your physical state to the state of pure thought, the whole of existence moves towards you – the heavens realign to catch your feet as you fall from an awareness of yourself as a corporeal being to an awareness of a Limitless and Eternal force.

Chapter Six
The Third Tier

The mind is the greatest enemy of the Seeker after Truth. Both mind and truth must be sacrificed at the edge of the black river to gain entrance into that which is real – that which exists outside of Maya. Thought is the interpretation of anything whatsoever, facilitated by mind, all interpretations relying on experiences gained not in any real circumstances, but gained instead in the world of falsehood created in a large part by the mind itself.

Mind cannot be trusted; it cannot be relied on to provide anything accurate, usable, or even pertinent. The Great Abyss that separates the realms of Soul from the worlds of Maya is the chaos of wrenching control away from the mind and its millions of faulty calculations and turning such awareness over to the experience itself. Likewise, "truth" cannot be trusted, as it is a subjective knowledge based on the aforementioned erroneous analysis of experience.

I spent some time in the abyss. In the moment of my projection from my physical body, I would find myself there. And the abyss followed me back through the silver cord to the earth, infesting my life with hopelessness. I have undergone a series of "dark nights of the soul," and this period was chief among them.

Yet I persisted, sure that if I Traveled to the other worlds, I would find a doorway out of the abyss, or the grace of some spiritual Master or another would release me, like Virgil allowing me to suffer in hell only long enough to more surely appreciate heaven.

No door was found, but instead a transformation, a transfiguration, in an instant passing through the abyss into the next world, into the next sphere, closer to the Source.

I closed my eyes, fixed my mind on the other worlds, and I jumped. Rather than falling back into the blackness of outer darkness to be surrounded by impermeable sorrow, I was instead soaring through liquid light. So fast was my Ascent that my ethereal skin burned, but I could not slow my flight. I could feel it tearing away from me like flesh from bones in Hiroshima. The sobbing that seemed to be made by the darkness of the abyss itself was replaced by the sound of fierce screaming, as a starving infant at a dead mother's breast. I was horrified, and longed for the solace of that black and hopeless perdition again, but my Ascent could not be slowed. I looked out, my three eyes burning, but insistent upon finding that shrieking babe, but saw only the liquid light, like a rampant river of living paint which passed through me as I flew.

As the last remains of my form were torn from me, like skin from muscle and muscle from bone, I realized that the screaming was coming from within myself. I was the babe, and indeed my mother had died, and the breast of life and identity and relation had withered under my incessant sucking.

Like a suicide jumper growing quietly comfortable with the previous rush of the fall a split-second before impact, the momentum of my flight was no longer startling, but instead I was able to observe it quite spectacularly. I was not flying upwards, nor was I plummeting down. I did not move from side to side. Instead, it was as if I was turning inside out, and at the same time expanding beyond myself, at such a rate to defy any conventional explanation of speed. And the thought came clearly, *I have no more form. What, then, am I?* My self having been stripped from me, what can identity be but pure power, unfettered by shape, thought, or even mind?

I looked around again at the rushing river of color, and there was no separation. I was not an object in the river, a boulder around which the waters parted, but I was the liquid light itself. And I flowed down as light and sound to the lower planes, revisiting the worlds that I had Traveled from, not descending into those lower forms, but delivering the light and the power of myself to them, as the light and power of the Eternal is delivered constantly.

And as if by an inhalation from that realm of light itself, I was drawn back up into the gulf of the liquid light. And with eyes that did not exist, I beheld the center of that World, a torso larger than I could fathom, arms outstretched, becoming the light, waist flowing down becoming the light, hair and eyes and ears and skin becoming that liquid light. From this single embodiment on that plane, all of the power of the Eternal flowed into the lower worlds, spurring into motion the quantum and the universal shifts that create form on the various planes of condensation.

My attention returned to myself, and I found that I was shrieking once more, wailing for my mother, the physical plane, the earth and the body that hung limp awaiting me. My eyes shot open and I gasped for air as if I hadn't tasted it for days, as if I had crawled out of a subterranean crypt and needed to feed my resurrected lungs. Before I could think to slowly reawaken my body to this world, I was standing, bolted up from the chair like it was rigged to a car battery, jumpstarting my heart. It took me several minutes of thrashing and gasping, slobbering on the carpeted floor and covering my eyes burning from the daylight before I was even able to recognize that I had returned to my body.

I looked at the clock. I had been in that other place for so long, for at least hours, if not longer. I had traveled further than any measurement of distance could calculate, beyond not only the reach of this universe, but beyond the reach of even thought itself. I had become the sea of creative flame of which and through which all things are created, and I had beheld the single embodiment on that plane. I had participated in the simultaneous acts of creation, sustentation, and destruction in the lower worlds, and rose again as that juggernaut Creator inhaled.

Only two minutes had elapsed.

Part III
Convergence

All of my work up to this point - every page that I have written, every interview that I have participated in, the seminars and workshops that I have conducted, and the individual mentoring I have provided for others – all has been to advance the conscious awareness of the process of spiritual Ascent. It has been my mandate to disseminate the message that the human being is Eternal, that each person is God, and can consciously access the states of Godhood whilst still incarnated in these bodies of flesh. It has been my struggle to lay out, or sometimes to simply hint at the methods that can be employed to such ends as discovering your own Eternal nature.

This task has been accomplished. The next rung must now be grasped.

It is one thing, in the safe confines of your inner vision and internal experience, to fly beyond the borders of space and time into the remaining dimensions of existence; it is quite another matter – a more dangerous, exhaustive, and potent feat – to bring the essence of those dimensions into this realm of three. Overlapping the planes in any conscious way deteriorates the walls between them, until your task is no longer to see and experience what lies beyond, but all of your effort is funneled towards simply surviving the experience.

In the state of Soul Travel, turning your attention back towards your body and forcing a sharp inhalation, you are instantly returned. The farther away from your body you travel, the more painful the re-entry is, but the point here is that within seconds you are able to escape the terror of the Lord of all Glory and return to the safety of these three familiar dimensions. Once you begin to bring those dimensions here, however, there is nowhere left to escape to. A sharp inhalation will prove only to strengthen the rift between the worlds and bring more clearly to your vision that which you are desperate to obfuscate.

The faux painter that I apprenticed under referred to the being that I had beheld at the center of creation as "Sat Nam." His statement of such was devoid of any explanation as to where that name had come from or what it meant. I adopted such as my only reference to this Creator.

When my studies moved into the use of mantra, that ancient name arose again: Sat Nam. Its meaning was then revealed as, "True Name," or "True Identity."

Again and again I Ascended through the planes of existence to dissolve my form into the sea of liquid light. I preferred that Home over the physical plane. Even my return and the slamming of my heart as if stopped during my travel became addictive. And again I would see the figure at the center of the pool of power, floating in its own magnificence, appearing each time more and more like the radiant creator, surrounded by seraphim, fiery ones, not embodied angels but living Flames.

Without moving its mouth, it would speak, a voice rumbling across the Formative Plane, heard not by ears that no longer existed, but passing through the tongues of light and piercing the intelligences of all who looked on.

The hours of conversation that I would carry on with the Spiritual Masters, either in their temples in other realms or in my home, were replaced by a few seconds in the presence of Sat Nam, all power and knowledge distilling into my being in the moment that I discarded form and image to become a simple current of light flowing from his center.

Each time I sat, closed my eyes, and began to move my consciousness away from the body and towards that Formative Plane, I prepared myself for the possibility that, in the process of tearing my mind away from Soul, which this journey could possibly be my last, that perhaps this would be the adventure from which I may not return. And as I approached that realm and heard the screaming infant within, terror grabbed my heart and squeezed.

Like jumping from a cliff into the cool water below, I would still jump from the cliff of consciousness into the everlasting pool of liquid light again and again, never sure if my body would be shattered by unseen rocky spires beneath the surface.

With each visit to Sat Nam, to that True Identity that I could at that point only witness subjectively, as if it existed somehow outside of myself, believing in the myth of separateness, I would flow out farther as It exhaled, and as it inhaled I would return even closer to its limitless body. As It breathed, I breathed, the breath and the life pulling me deeper into the whirlwind of flames surrounding Sat Nam.

With one particular inhalation on one particular visit, the separation ceased. The voice shook the worlds all around: *Become Sat Nam.* There was no flooding into that body, no juxtaposition with it, there was only the simple becoming, the realization of *my* True Identity. I looked out of those Eternal eyes to see my vaporous arms and legs flowing into the worlds below, the rays of light streaming from my fiery pupils giving it form, the exhalations from my lips breathing life into every electron in the worlds below. Creation is not a thing that happened once upon a time; creation is happening at all times, and if the process were to ever halt, so would all that is created.

My travels to the Formative Plane became a task not of getting there or of becoming Sat Nam, but it all became like a game or a test that I would apply to myself, to see how long I could sustain the outwards churning of all power through me, how long I could remain as the creator. All of this was experienced quite unconsciously, plugging myself into the center of a process that I could not even comprehend.

After several months of growing accustomed to being Sat Nam - although "being" It was more like witnessing It from the inside - I found that I would occasionally open my eyes to return to the earth without the deep and sharp breath in, to return my life to that body. In doing so, a part of me was still in that state, was still Sat Nam, while my mind had returned to my flesh and was able to translate the ongoing experience. The panic that set in forced that deep and sharp inhalation and brought my essence back into my body, but I began to wonder what would happen if I instead remained in that state, remained as Sat Nam while my physical eyes were opened, while walking this world as a man.

At first, it seemed like some sort of bi-location, where a part of my consciousness was galaxies away as the creator while the majority of myself was operating the organic machine on this earth. With repetition, however, the separation dissolved even more, and I realized that God's Throne upon which I could be seated was not in some distant place, but was right below me, and that all that was necessary was to sink into it. Gradually, the experience became not as a secret bi-location, but instead took on the form of God in the body of a man, living out the petty instances of humanity, smiling internally as if a child hiding behind semi-translucent curtains.

Now and again, those who looked closely at those curtains could see Sat Nam behind my eyes, and could hear Its voice within my words, especially when the idea of veiling this truth had slipped my mind, usually when conversing on subjects of spirituality. The mantra that these accidental observers would repeat was, "I don't know if I should run away from you screaming or towards you sobbing." Such was always my own predicament in approaching that dreaded True Identity.

Powers proceeded to fall upon me, abilities, which the yogis would call Siddhis; abilities beyond the normal human experience. Supernormal abilities were not alien to me, as I had for most of my life played with their attainment, and then once attained had tested their limits at every chance, but these new Siddhis were different mainly in their automatic nature. I did not ask directly for these powers, nor would I consciously attempt to utilize them, but instead found that sometimes in the most inopportune moments I would receive glimpses of the intentions, the history, or the focus of those around me. This was quite unlike any sort of telepathy or empathy; it was not as if I were seeing into the minds of these people, but instead as if I were seeing into their souls.

My ability to manifest events and objects in my life was multiplied, to the degree that dwelling on any desire, with a greater-than-usual amount of emotion, would bring the object of such desire hurling through space towards me. The effects of my rituals were also amplified and the speed at which their goals were achieved was cut down to sometimes minutes.

The more that I was able to consciously enter the Sat Nam state and pull the awareness of that state into the senses of this body, the more it seemed that I was nearing the endless power of that Creator.

Along with the various Siddhis that I was developing, a certain awareness was being distilled in me as well. This awareness began as a simple, silent knowledge of the presence of spiritual beings around me, or the sensation of the swelling of powerful forces in my environment. Before I was given time to assimilate this awareness into any sort of cognitive process, those things that I had previously only been aware of started to emerge into this world. At the forty-five degree angle, between my vision's periphery and my active sight, I would see figures, people, standing where they had not been moments before, or colored ripples on my screen of vision, as if the ocean of liquid light was pressing up against this world and trying to melt a hole into it. The conversations with spiritual beings that were normally reserved for seated silence instead occurred in everyday situations, their voices coming from previously empty air, or their ethereal bodies materializing beside me.

I found myself daily putting into practice the various tests to determine if these visions were indeed visions, or if I was simply falling into a sudden insanity. All things were verified, all trademarks of authentic vision accounted for. But the gap between this world and the other was decreasing, disappearing even.

I cannot remember the day that it happened, the exact moment when the veil was lifted completely. Within months, however, I went from having to sit in meditation and ritual in order to view the spiritual worlds and interact with them to instead seeing both worlds simultaneously, as of two semitransparent worlds overlapping one another. I don't recall at what point I quit living life as a person, but I found that I had left my job, thrown away all of my possessions save for a handful of books and a bag of clothes, and had moved out of the house that I was renting to instead wander the steaming streets in the desert sun with glossed eyes scanning the overlap between the worlds.

The ocean of liquid light was upon me, around me. The sidewalks melted into color and the air vaporized into flames. In the sea of light, people passing appeared as lights slightly brighter than the sea, like glowing jellyfish or metallic scales reflecting the sunlight. As I exhaled, I swept as a current of motion outwards, into the sea, into the light around me, and each breath in brought me back to the center of existence.

Unshaven, dirty, with wild eyes and wilder hair, sleeping in cemeteries where only the dead could disturb me, after a month or two of twenty-four hours a day of ecstasy, it occurred to me that this simply could not be sustained.

Translation from the flesh and from this life that held it was the only alternative to building partitions in my experience, manufacturing a shut-off valve in my own soul to stop the flow of power and knowledge.

Sitting in a city park, a couple of kids kicking a soccer ball back and forth in the center, some city workers installing irrigation pipes around the periphery, I sat with my back against a tree. I breathed in, my intention to leave that other world and to ground myself in this one causing the overlap to fade. Each breath drew me further away from that place of power and solidified my existence in this prison of pain, a sob choking me, that same feeling you get as you walk out on a lover with your suitcase in your hand. With what I knew would be my final breath out of that unending glory, I called the name of Suhnam. Just as the vision of the worlds beyond closed like a door and the vacuum sucked the beauty beyond the hinges with it, my Master appeared beside me.

My vision blurred with tears, I asked him to help me put my life back together, to regain all that I had given up.

"Stretch your hand towards the earth, and speak, and it will blossom."

I stretched my hand, and all over my power, towards this world, towards my goals, one by one, discharging furious and vengeful bursts of intention, unhampered by the sort of disbelief that would never be possible for me again.

With minimal physical effort, a new job was provided for me, and then a car, and a new house. And I would return into those other worlds, but like a heroin addict going to a methadone clinic, I had to pace myself for a while until I knew that I could control my urge to forget again this world in favor of that other.

Chapter Seven
Commanding Convergence

The simplest spiritual exercise that I have ever learned to use has also become the most powerful weapon in my arsenal.

The legend of the Messiah makes the claim that Jesus was able to feed four thousand people with seven loaves of bread and a few fishes on one occasion, and then repeated the miracle with five thousand people using only two fish and two loaves[1].

Similar myths have circulated concerning the so-called Master Count of Saint Germain, a mysterious figure in the mid 1700s who was thought to be an alchemist and a spiritual Master. The transmutation of base elements seemed to be second-nature for Saint Germain, turning lead into gold and causing impure gems to repair their own flaws, without the aid of any material other than a silk cloth placed over the item. More impressively, the Count was said to be able to cause gems to multiply themselves beneath the cloth, as well as to bring into physical reality objects which had previously existed only in the imagination.

My own mentor, Baba Maharaja, was followed by such rumors. While I stayed in his home, a small group of disciples who had traveled with Raj from India, into Africa, across Asia, and to the United States would gather every few days to discuss the teachings of this great man, and, seemingly more pressing, to gossip.

One tale that I heard from several different disciples was that, in India, Raj gathered up all of his followers and told them to drop what they were doing and walk with him into the desert. Raj informed them that they would likely be gone for a few days, but instructed them to bring water only. There were obvious protests, as the disciples had no issue with a vigorous hike, nor with prolonged fasting, but combining the two seemed to guarantee illness and death. Their concerns were simply dismissed, and the call to join the walk was reiterated.

At the end of the first day's hike through the searing desert heat, the group stopped for the night. Rather than letting everyone slump down and relax, Baba Maharaja told them to pile as much sand as they could into any one spot, creating a mound of desert sand. In their retellings, most of Raj's disciples would lower their voices as to not be overheard making mention of their contempt for their guru, as he seemed unscathed by the solar heat, by the dry air blowing down his throat and into his eyes, or by the lack of food through such an intense hike. Nevertheless, as he instructed, his disciples did. Once the sand had been piled into a heap a few feet tall, Raj climbed to the peak of it and sat, legs folded, wrists resting on his knees, his spine straight, and without any declaration to the group, he began to chant a single sound, a Bija Mantra, one flowing song carried by that dry wind across the forsaken desert. The disciples sat in their own postures around the mound of sand, forming a circle surrounding it, and joined him in the song.

Every time that this story was told to me, each orator would add, with almost choked and cracking voices, how their concern for hunger, discomfort, exhaustion, even their thirst and the needs of their body evaporated as they sang that one syllable over and over, letting the drone of it fill their entire being. All of their needs and desires were replaced with an unmatchable peace.

This, in itself, was inspiring to me, to think of following a guru into the desert without any preparations, placing all of my faith in him to not only keep me safe, but to keep me alive, and then to discover absolute serenity after breaking down the conflict of the mind and the body.

After meditating for what seemed to be a few hours, though, Baba Maharaja stopped chanting, lifting his head as if waking from a long sleep, and stumbled off of the pile of sand. The disciples sat, filled with love and peace so fierce that resuming any sort of physical action seemed intolerable.

With a hint of confusion in his voice, an inflection that gave the impression that he didn't know any more about what they were doing there than any of his followers, he told them to replace the sand into the desert, and that they would go home.

As the group of disciples lifted handfuls of sand from the pile to scatter back into the desert, there were shrieks of excitement and even disbelief. Just beneath the surface layer of sand – the very sand that they had piled there themselves only hours earlier, and had not left unattended for even a moment – there was a pile of fresh fruit.

And so, with not even a fish, not even a loaf, but with a pile of sand, Baba Maharaja fed the masses.

These stories and the thousands of others that I've come across in my quest for the Eternal never did leave me amazed or in awe at the power of that individual, but instead left me asking, *How can I do this? What is the formula?*

My search turned to alchemy, but instead of the instantaneous transmutation or even transubstantiation of the elements, I found either New Age wishful thinking or simple metallic and mineral chemistry.

My desire was not to learn to mix compound A with catalyst B and filter through C in order to arrive at D, nor was it to see the glory of God in the everyday suffering and torment of the human being. My desire, my intention, was and is to bring the fullness of the power of the Eternal into this plane, into these hands, to work the miraculous and to align the currents of causality to bring about my Will.

As I studied the deepest doctrines of the occult and the most esoteric rites of the religions, the answer to my question of *how can I have this power* eluded me. I could perform minor miracles, through ritual sorcery or through spirit communication, but to create spontaneously, to take such an absolute minimum base substance as sand or fish, and to materialize as much abundance as was needed was far from my grasp.

As in all endeavors, the moment that I stopped looking was the same moment that the answer was delivered to me.

Baba Maharaja, who for quite some time after leaving his immediate tutelage, remained a guide in the shadows of my life for the past decade, and who has seen me and helped me through several transitions and transfigurations, was the one who the Eternal spoke through to me, to grant me the most simple piece of knowledge, the most obvious formula that would change my life and my world.

This same knowledge, which was once a secret, has now seemingly been revealed to many as the time for full revelation falls upon the earth. The formula below, in the years following my learning it from Baba Maharaja has since been uttered from the mouths of Hindu Masters, Yogis, and even regurgitated by self-help psychologists who have no concept of the limitless power that they hold not in their hands, but on their lips.

All of creation exists as a continuous harmony, as one song composed of countless sounds, bound together by a melody which breathes every particle into reality. At the finest and most subtle levels of any thing, there is no difference between one and another, no spatial or temporal separation, no division between this and that. All that keeps reality from pooling as gelatinous ooze is the eternal song that vibrates from within the core elements of each different thing. The individual arias do not create only separation, though; it is this universal song which gives reality its form and binds the parts together as a whole.

There are sounds within this universal song that, when isolated, are found to resonate as an undercurrent in each individual sound, creating a concurrent melody capable of inciting very particular reactions in not only the immediate subject, but also in the whole fabric of existence through the web of the song.

The formation of mantras, prayers, hymns, and the wide variety of various spiritual vocalizations are aimed at appealing to this universal song. More and more elaborate sound combinations and rhythms have been constructed to produce this effect, when in reality the most simple sounds are those which will cause the elements to shift and all of creation to move.

These are the sounds by which the growth of our universe was seeded, called in that old and magical tongue of Sanskrit, "Bija Mantra." Contrasting with the varied and musical pronunciations of the gayatri and initiatory mantras, the formative seed sounds consist of a single syllable, and require the most minimal vocal effort. The power of the Bija Mantra, again in extreme contrast to nearly every other type of oration, does not lie in the intention or exertion of the orator, but in the song itself.

Entering the space between the worlds, between the waking state and the Awakened state, in that theta-gamma sync, the Bija Mantras activate specific aspects of Godhood within you, quite spontaneously. Through Bija Mantra Yoga alone, all Siddhis will flow through you.

HAUM attunes the lower self to the needs of the greater self, even of the God Self. Repetition of this mantra for twenty-four minutes – one minute for each hour of the day – will speed up the rate of Ascent, will carry you into supernal bliss, and will align all events and circumstances in your daily life to set you on your own Dharmic path.

UHL, which can be made by pressing the tongue to the roof of the mouth and allowing the sound of the letter L escape in a continuous drone, thrusts you not into the highest states of glory, but instead centers you in the sea of energy that surrounds you, the currents of power parting around you. In this state, nearly every lower occult Operation, in basic energy manipulation, thought-insertion, and assertion of will, is manifested instantly. All of the power sought after for lifetimes by Sorcerers is yours within moments.

AHM, made by pressing the lips together and allowing the south of the letter M to escape in a continuous drone awakens the full potential of the Sahasrara, or Crown, Chakra. If the pituitary gland, which is associated with the Sahasrara Chakra, has been dormant and neglected, the first two or three sessions of chanting AM will seem like twenty-four minutes of indescribable internal torture. A breaking point is reached soon after, however, when the physical and spiritual encrustations are shattered and euphoria washes over your whole being. There is no faster way to attainment of what is often called Christ Consciousness, or Supersoul Awareness, than the full and constant activation of the Sahasrara Chakra, and this single Bija Mantra unlocks the door to that thousand-petaled lotus.

While there are dozens of these seed sounds recorded, and hundreds more yet to be revealed, the one with which we are concerned here is the sound of creation, seemingly *ex nihilio*. This is the mantra that Baba Maharaja used when transmuting grains of sand into fruit. This is the song that Sat Nam gives to bring the universe into form out of formlessness.

If you have never before attempted meditation, performed a single spiritual operation of any sort, or have yet to experience any of the mystical wonders that I have journaled in this work, then this single meditation will elevate you beyond your expectations of connectedness to and immersion in the spiritual worlds. For those Adepts who put into practice this most simple meditation, greater degrees of godhood will be unveiled.

Seated wherever you like, in any position, at any hour, facing any direction, bring your awareness to the center of your forehead, your Ajna Chakra, the Third Eye which holds all power and beholds all knowledge. Feel the tension in this spot, as if all of the power of godhood within you is trapped behind this closed door. The more attention that you bring to this energy center, the more pronounced and frustrating the blockage will seem, until you find yourself near screaming to be released. At this moment of critical mass, when the energy behind the closed door of the Ajna Chakra has reached its peak, divert a portion of your focus to the area of your perineum, where yet another Chakra, another energetic center of your being lies, where all of your desire, need, drive, and instinct is generated and filtered up into the branches and leaves of your being.

In the moment that your attention is placed onto this root energy center, the muscles there will seem to instantly and automatically contract. What you are then left with is the feeling of one energy center at the lowest part of your main body contracting and pushing upwards while the energy center at the highest part of your body pulsates and pushes outwards. You have become a funnel through which the power of the gods may siphon through you into the universe as a whole.

In this state alone it is possible to become Shiva or Brahma, to create and to destroy, to wipe away the world as it stands and to erect a new one on its ashes. The power flowing through you, although literally omnipotent, is unformed, a shockwave released from that Third Eye into the world, ready to obliterate or to sanctify, at random. It is the Bija Mantra which will mold this power and will direct it. It is through this simple song that all of creation will attune to your desire and will recompose reality.

Without disrupting the current of power flowing through you, from your root to your release, inhale slowly, deeply, and as the breath naturally leaves your throat, allow sound to be carried with it. With no motion from your tongue, no contraction of your throat or positioning of your lips, allowing the breath of life to escape you and to deliver sound from within, the only sound that can be made is AH. AH, the reverence of the Almighty. AH, the release of Bindu into the womb of the world. AH, the giving up of concern, the relinquishing of worry, and the acceptance of the inevitable return.

Again, breathe in, and as you breathe out, direct the air to travel more slowly through your body, more steadily, carrying that most natural song from your lips. The gates are flung open and from that Third Eye spills all power as the song fills the air: AHHH.

Fold the universe upon itself in order to connect that which you desire to that which you possess, to connect that which will be to that which is. Hold in your mind the image of that future state, feeling your lust for it clenched in your root energy center, released through the column of power, spiraling towards your forehead, the desire itself wrapped in the wings of a thousand angels, carried to all corners of existence.

One minute for each hour of the day, twenty-four minutes you should endure the glory, even though within the first ten repetitions of the Bija Mantra all separation between wanting and having have ceased. For twenty-four minutes, become the Creator.

This is far too simple to work, to actually produce results. Where are the candles, the sigils, the incantations, and circumambulations?

All that I desired began to pour into my life, chasing after me as I meditated in this manner upon those things, taking my lust for them and turning it into a tangible flow of fluid force. The most difficult manifestations, those things which I knew that my dealings with the lower forces of the occult could not gather for me were brought to me within weeks. The weeks shortened into days. The days became minutes, as I would often have a knock on the door or the ringing of a telephone disrupt my meditation as I neared twenty-four minutes, the voice or the personage at the other end of the disruption bringing news of the success of the Operation that had yet to be completed.

Time will soon no longer exist if it were to be measured by the space between that which I desire and the attainment of it. I have not turned a pile of sand into fruit, nor have I materialized fish and loaves, but in my own life I have witnessed miracles comparable to, if not greater than these.

This is not magick. This is miracle.

Chapter Eight

Omnipotence

I am the Gate through which I must pass into Eternity.
I am the silent contemplation that is the key to that Gateway. I
am the words of the Secret Mantra, and the voice of the one
who sings. I am Eternity, I am Eternal.
    I am the constant turning of the Wheel of Eighty-Four.
I am the Eternal unfolding of Soul. I am the Voice of God,
Shabda, proceeding forth from the Divine without end.
    - Taken from E.A. Koetting's Personal Journal of Meta-
physical Experimentation, entry 11/09/2003.

    Although I had learned the secret and ancient formulas
of the occult, the various rituals, summonings, incantations,
and the ritual methods used to summon forth every spirit, force,
and phenomenon, it was not until I temporarily abandoned the
occult sciences and returned to the religion of my upbringing,
the Church of Jesus Christ of Latter-Day Saints, that I was
forced to learn how to manifest the miraculous without such
methods.
    The LDS Church believes that its founder, Joseph
Smith, received from the Godhead, from angels that ministered

to him, and from a series of books collectively compiled on golden plates which were revealed to him by these angels the Church of Jesus Christ, as He had created it during his mortal life on earth. All of the power of the Godhead operated on earth through the Priesthood, which is received in two parts. The first priesthood, called the Priesthood of Aaron, the brother of Moses, is now given to boys at the age of twelve. Through the Aaronic Priesthood, the priesthood holder is able to teach and convert, to prepare, bless, and distribute the holy sacraments of bread and water, divine flesh and blood, to the worthy, and to call upon the ministering of angels.

The second priesthood, the Priesthood of Melkezedek, allows the priesthood holder to "act as the mouthpiece of god." Through the holder of the Melkezedek Priesthood, who must be eighteen years old, morally clean, and active in the congregation, the will of God can be delivered through blessings and through revelation. The Melkezedek Priesthood holder is also able to call upon divine authority to perform miracles, heal the sick, raise the dead, and even to command the gates of heaven to open and to step through them.

The rich kaleidoscope mythologies revolving around the central recognition of the figure and fable of the man who has become known as Jesus Christ seems to me at times never as lustrous as it is within the Church of Jesus Christ of Latter-Day Saints, although I'm certain the same is held by former members for their own previous childhood religions. As I left the Mormon Church and embraced the occult in my early pre-pubescence, I disregarded the myth as nothing more substantial than that, and went on my way searching for vision, power, and substantiation of the spiritual through magick.

My body, mind, and emotions worn thin and run ragged through my descent into the blackest rites and the most depraved lifestyle, I sought a re-emergence into the sunlight, into a world where hope, kindness, and love were not considered to be vices. The emergency exit was lit not by a green, glowing sign, but instead by a bright, glowing girl who offered herself to me if I would return to the LDS Church. Like a lamb to the slaughter, confusing a more delicate prison for some sort of freedom, I followed.

Once inside this new world wherein I was not allowed to wield my million swords of knowledge and power, I was drawn across the paths of others who knew power, but who had never used ritual of any sort.

I had seen the Melkizedek priesthood in use through my life, mainly on occasions, rites of passage, and other events where it seemed appropriate to invoke that priesthood. I had never before, however, witnessed its use as those within the Church with whom I aligned myself used it.

The memorized words given by the church to conduct such a priesthood blessing were, on the lips of these servants, perfunctory only in the beginning, only to establish their spiritual authority, after which I observed a definite lapsing-out, a blanking out of expression, a glazing over in the eyes, all thought, all memorization, all concern for ridicule washed away by the spiritual force that then entered. The Holy Spirit invoked, the lips then moved without the brain's command, the words flowing out halting and assuming a strange cadence as if the orator attempted to decipher some alien tongue.

And with the stream of unthought words flowed ungenerated power, a force filling the whole body and discharging through the hands laid on the head of the receiver, and a humble yet tremendous love, heartbreaking and healing at the same time. Everyone in the room could feel it; even the most skeptical could not deny that *something* was occurring outside of the normal realm of communication.

I witnessed, through these blessings, the miraculous healing of ancient illnesses, the instant setting of bones, the dissolution of a multitude of obstacles in the lives of the blessed. And then I took that invisible and intangible scepter in my hand and I blessed others likewise, my lips uttering blessings that my brain had not conceived, my soul pouring forth power as automatic as the words, and I witnessed miracles passing into this world through my hands.

Then there was one soldier of spirit, a fringe-dweller within the church, a giant in physical as well as spiritual stature. Reese would raise his arm to the square, palm facing away from him. His powerful body would visibly weaken, his head would droop in the moment that his mind went blank, and that Holy Spirit would ride through him, the words he spoke not his but another's, the words spoken by the legions of angels surrounding him, issued now from his own lips. As he taught me through his example how to use this priesthood in the most profound ways, he and I became as two prophets wandering the cities hidden in the desert, flooding the skies with blessings, concerned not for what could be delivered to us for our benefit, but reveling in the changes occurring around us, through our own relinquishing of even the desire to be credited for our miracles.

The secret to the power was not in the supposed Keys of the Priesthood, but instead was in the ability to shut off my mind and to allow a greater intellect to speak through me. By my own power, my force and my thought, I could do nothing. As a conduit for the Eternal, however, my power was limitless.

When my journey in the Church of Jesus Christ of Latter-Day Saints came to a close, transitioned by my own experiences in Soul Travel, it was this lesson that I left with, that of dropping the mind yet allowing the body to continue to function and interact through commands given by an intelligence surpassing that which is funneled through the brain.

Power is a tricky thing, in that the discipline, the purity of intention, the singular focus, and the relinquishing of your own mind and will to the direction of the intelligence and Will of the God Self often precludes carrying through most changes that you had originally desired to enact through your godlike power. With the simple glamours and spells available in just about any occult booklet, this preclusion is not so direct nor so intense, but it builds as your power builds, as your Ascent builds, as you move towards that omnipotent state, until you find once you hold all power that you have concomitantly lost all desire to use that power.

I have sat countless times in deep meditation, in Soul Travel even, rising to the heights of the Formative Plane, becoming Sat Nam, becoming the God Self, and upon return to my body, I have carried a portion of that godhood with me, back into this realm. And in such a state, I have looked out into the visible streaks of sunlight and the wind stirring fragile branches, and have heard the critters scurrying around my body in the soil, and I have known, without any reservation, that the command could be given from my lips to blacken the sun, and it would blacken. This knowledge was never a matter of pride or ego – at least not until much later, when mind had returned to evaluate the experience – but it was always a matter of fact.

When your form dissolves into pure power and expands into every electron in existence, when your mind is thrown off of you and leaves you with *understanding* where thought used to play, an understanding that reaches beyond time and past all boundaries into an intimate knowledge of all that is, you are stricken dumb by the realization that there is no separation between things, that there is no difference, at all. The same force that can be used to heal the sick or to remove an enemy from your path can just as readily be invoked to extinguish a star. There is no difference.

If you possess power, which you surely do, as all things do because there is no separation between anything and anything else; and if the reality of the existence of the Eternal Source is sure, and therefore there is no difference between any one thing and the Source of All Things; *since* you possess power in any measure, to accomplish any minute task through nonphysical means, then you verily possess *all* power to accomplish *any* task. One is not more difficult than the other, in any real way.

Manifested existence is not experienced in a spiritual vacuum, however, and so the gross and lower forces, internal and external, form invisible barriers that must be shed in order to access the highest faculties of the human being. Chief among these barriers, as has already been elucidated throughout this text, is that of the mind.

It was always a simple task for me to manifest money through nonphysical means, initially through the occult. I would light silver and blue candles and would push out of my every Chakra and my every pore my intention to receive money. I would request of the elements and the watchtowers, and later of the angels and the demons, in some rhyming and lyrical manner, to bring me money. Usually within a day I'd come across the exact amount of money that I needed, without promise of repayment or even a request for thanks.

Two or three hundred dollars seemed to be the ceiling of my ability to manifest. I could believe that the forces of spirituality could bring me this small amount of money, but that some karmic offense would be taken to requesting more, or to even imagining it possible to receive more than that.

As I spent more and more time in the Formative Plane, not as myself, the self that I have learned to call "myself," but instead as Sat Nam, as my True Identity, as that Eternal entity who *is* power and knowledge and presence, I suffered the most strange malady of a complete lack of disbelief. I became a madman, convinced that anything is possible, even probable, and that *I* could induce that "anything" into materialization.

On April 15th, 2003, I manifested three thousand dollars for a friend of mine, delivered to her within three days after performing the basic ritual – a ritual I had used time and again to collect enough money for a pack of cigarettes, a soda, and a hamburger.

Rather than jumping and dancing at this success, at this leap in my personal, spiritual evolution, it instead quieted me, vindicating that which I had already known.

I have summoned much larger amounts of money for myself and for others. Alas, my desire to use this power faded in the very instant of its attainment.

I have postulated, more in conversations with myself than with any other person that the reason prophets are not calling fire down from the heavens or turning cities to salt anymore is because it is not deemed necessary. Instead, we produce more subtle miracles that are more fitting to our needs.

It had only been necessary for me, until that day in April, to materialize a few dollars here and there. It wasn't until I was called on to produce much more that I found myself capable of doing so. That capability was not invoked in that moment, but was merely lying latent and awaiting the appropriate catalyst.

When it later became necessary to possess much, much larger amounts of money, those came to me just as easily.

When imprisoned, specifically in April of 2003 on several quite serious felonies, without much hope of release for some time, I stretched my hand to the concrete walls and that voice came from me again, commanding them to crumble so that I may walk into the streets free. Within seconds after the pronouncement, I was released, and all charges were dismissed. When all of the forces of negation seemed to compound against me, I have become untouchable. When need arises, it is nearly instantly fulfilled. The same power that Reese had taught me to use to bless others was easily perverted or manipulated, directed towards whatever goal presented itself in the moment. By releasing desire, releasing all sense of limitation, and simply speaking the words of my will, miracles have flooded out before me.

It is a stretch of the most obscene sort to compare summoning any amount of money, or gaining any favors of the lower worlds, to the same omnipotence that is used to fashion from an ocean of nothingness the universes, and then to destroy them and create them again anew, but such is an illustration of boundaries that the mind creates between the power that is within us all and the achievement of the ends towards which that power is directed.

Like enlightenment, moments of omnipotence - or more accurately, moments of the realization of your own omni-potence – are indeed moments. They float by, and sometimes we can catch them, if our own breath does not blow them away from us. We can hold them for a second or two, as a gift from our Self to ourselves, and then mind returns and scolds us for such silliness. And then, as if we are all babes, the veil is drawn again over our eyes, and we forget that we are God.

Chapter Nine
Omnipresence

I sat with Master Suhnam in my living room, on my beige sofa embroidered with images of nondescript flowers.

"Turn your attention inwards," he guided me as my eyelids fluttered closed in the initial stages of this meditation. "Focus upon your breath, and upon bindu."

As my attention moved inwards and I focused upon that single invisible and intangible spot where a third eye might appear, I was drawn without further intention or focus into a state of Soul Travel, unique however, in that I did not travel anywhere at all, but remained in the room, exactly where I had been within my body, only in those more subtle and more powerful bodies, looking around my house with fresh, eternal eyes.

Suhnam motioned towards a vase that sat on a wall shelf. "Become the vase."

My experience in the Formative Plane had carved in my understanding my ability to dissolve my form completely and become the liquid light around me. I likewise dissolved my form and as that pure light I entered the vase, my energy and my intelligence filling the pores and the ceramic with as little

E.A. Koetting

effort as flowers and water required to fill the cavity of the vase itself.

"Become the vase," Suhnam repeated, his voice assuming a peculiar conviction. "Do not fill the vase; do not enter the vase – become the vase."

His command brought me back to the awareness of myself as a body, as a human, rather than a liquid intelligence and energy. I was back in my body.

I relaxed my mind again, refocused my attention on the vase, and poured myself once more into it. As I had on the Formative Plane, I released my mind and its millions of minute observations. I melted into the particles of the vase, no distinction remaining between where my ethereal body began and where the ceramic molecules of the vase ended. I could not see, because vases cannot see. I could not hear, because vases cannot hear. I could not think, as vases cannot think.

I was timeless, the substance of my ceramic body having been collected from the earth rather than born from the combination of genes.

My memory holds no recollection of the passage of time while I was the vase, nor do I remember having any concern for the idea of time, as vases are not concerned about the hour. For a long while, however, I was silently and blissfully a vase, the simplicity of that incarnation a welcome relief contrasted with the self-imposed megaton pressure of the human state.

Sorrow was the prime emotion upon my return to my body, my return to being a human. As a vase, there was no struggle, no battles with the mind and the heart, no concern for sustenance and shelter, not even a thought of existence, for vases do not think, "I am."

Suhnam motioned towards three separate items in different locations in the living room. "Become the clock, the plant, and the table." With the lessons learned from becoming the vase, I entered the clock and became it, dwelling in the rhythm of my moving hands and the tremors each of those movements trembling through my hollow, wooden torso. Rather than returning to my body, when I departed from the clock, I straightway entered the plant and became the plant, each leaf and stem with the same mind, no one part thinking or acting with autonomy, but the whole organism of my green and brown body forming an automatic collective. I then jumped from the plant into the table, my thin but strong legs solid beneath the polished surface of my back, the covering cloth and placemats laying on me like clothes.

I rushed back to my body, and regaining my awareness of myself and the ten thousand thoughts and emotions entailed, I was quite proud of myself for having so efficiently and exactly completed the task.

Suhnam looked disappointed. "You were to become all three objects," he said. "Not one after the other."

I sat puzzled. Did he really expect me to become all three objects at the *same time*? Why, that's not possible! Is it? At the very worst, I could attempt the feat in order to prove to my Master its impossibility.

With an exhalation from my lungs, I jumped from my body and instantly dissolved my ethereal form, becoming liquid light. As I grouped my nebulous self into three parts and headed into three directions, I heard that infant scream from all around as my mind and awareness were torn beyond their limits. The screaming sound remained as I entered the clock, the plant, and the table, and the sound blended into a buzzing and a singing as of a thousand choirs singing in sweet victory as I became each of those objects, simultaneously. The ecstasy of the experience was overwhelming, mirroring that which I had experienced on the Formative Plane as Sat Nam. Three objects, different in location, design, and composition, all infused with my consciousness, my disembodied intelligence, my Soul.

I returned to my body enlivened with the possibilities of this new multidirectional travel.

Suhnam directed me in becoming then my entire house, and then the neighborhood and all things and people within it. On and on I expanded, until I found myself above creation, back in the Formative Plane which had become my home, becoming every particle and wave and thought in existence, both in the physical plane and in those realms beyond, where form exists in more subtle substance.

Omnipresence is the state of being in all places at once. A step deeper into the understanding of omnipresence is the realization that in order to be in all places at once, the subject must therefore be *within* all things at once, and must in a way *be* all things at once. The principle Divine characteristics of omniscience, omnipotence, and omnipresence are the true trinity of the theistic state, and not one of these characteristics can exist without the others. The ability to expand your consciousness into every thing in existence would both require and would lend to omnipotence, as the sum of the power and ability of all things would equal to complete power; and such an expansion, and more importantly the sustaining of the omnipresent state, would require omniscience, and once held, being within all things, and *being* all things would deliver unto the subject all knowledge.

To be God, to enter the God State wherein omnipresence, omnipotence, and omniscience are fully realized requires a definite absence of the human mind. The name, the number, and the form of God are incomprehensible to the human mind, ineffable and incalculable. We must, therefore, take on a greater intelligence, a greater mind, the mind and understanding of the Divine, which is without limitation, as the Eternal is Limitless.

There is a paradox in the statement that you must at the same time drop mind, while expanding consciousness. What is consciousness if it is not mind, or if it at least is not connected to mind? In fact, it is not the consciousness that is expanded, being the awareness of the self as a microcosm in relation to the greater macrocosm, but instead it is the identity of the spiritual self that needs to be expanded. In that expansion, however, in the states of omnipresence, omnipotence, and omniscience, the individual comes to the stark realization that there is no individual soul, there is no "spiritual self" to be expanded, but that such is a very solid metaphor used as a tool to enter into the awareness of the boundlessness of all things. If you can expand yourself into everything, in all places at once, what is being expanded, and did it ever exist in a minute form? This is all Maya, a trick we play on ourselves, to believe that we are separate from that which surrounds us, and therefore necessitates our entrance into those objects, spaces, and psyches.

With repetition, it is realized without exception that you are not entering into objects apart from yourself, nor are you expanding into an endless space outside, but that you are transferring your awareness into another part of your own Eternal body.

The task, then, becomes not leaving your body and expanding your Self into all things, because this is indeed the natural state of man – Godhood is the natural state of man – but instead the task becomes collapsing the identity into a single form, reversing the expansion and containing the all powerful, all present, and all knowing self in a limited, singular, and confused body and mind. And thus, the transmigratory experience is recognized as the true experience of humanity, cloaked by illusions of separation and smallness, and the antitransmigratory experience begins.

Chapter Ten
Omniscience

Flickering like a golden flame through the kingdoms of the Astral Plane, through the quiet chaos of the causal, and alighting upon the sapphire streets of the mental plane, I was called by the Master there towards an iridescent lapis lazuli temple. There were no doors, although I cannot say that the entrance to the Temple lay open, some imperceptible membrane exorcising all uninvited from the threshold.

In the same moment that I crossed that threshold, the Master appeared at my side, a diminutive elder, hunched and slow.

"This is the house of the Akashic Records," his voice came, not from his mouth but from the visible aura that surrounded him.

What I actually saw in that moment I cannot describe, for upon my return to my body my brain had no references upon which to draw in order to make sense of the scene. That meaty tool instead concocted a memory of endless, glass file cabinets. As I drew each drawer open along its gliders, the paper files that I had expected to be there had been replaced with phosphorescent crystal shards. Placing the shards to my Ajna Chakra, I found that each crystal possessed an incredible amount of information, and that the data contained therein and the *first hand experience* of that information, all of which was delivered into my mind in the instant of contacting the crystal with that clairvoyant chakra. Each file cabinet represented a different subject or area of knowledge that can be absorbed by the mind, each section of file cabinets belonging to even more general categorizations of information.

I opened the cabinet concerning previous incarnations and pressed the crystal to my forehead. Rather than stopping at my skin or skull, as any object of matter would do in the physical plane, the crystal shard passed through my ethereal skin and embedded into whatever non-physical mind-center existed inside of my mental body's head. With a jarring convulsion of my mental body, and probably my physical body as well, I was assaulted by a million visions and experiences from different lives, possibly lived by the life force and identity that I have in this incarnation learned to call "myself." I slammed the crystal back into the file cabinet and slid it shut, ensuring that the latch had caught, as to not mistakenly release the same assault on myself or anyone else by carelessness.

For weeks following, the information that was within that crystal shard distilled into my active consciousness, forming memories from hundreds and thousands of years past, and some further back than that. My every dream and imagination, awake or asleep, became a visual recalling of the information that I had absorbed. Sickened by the amount and the intensity of the knowledge, I ceased all Soul Travel until the last vestiges of the information had worked through my brain.

And then I returned, to repeat.

Although such an experience on the Mental Plane can easily be mistaken for omnipresence, it is not. Accessing such cogs of the spiritual machinery can be useful and quite enlightening, but unlike the divine attributes of omnipresence, omnipotence, and omniscience, this simple access to portions of knowledge and power and presence *is not* enlightenment itself.

The first-hand experience of omniscience is nearly indistinguishable from omnipresence, as true omniscience is the inner and intimate knowledge of **all** things, in the same moment. Like omnipresence, you cannot simply experience the full knowledge of one subject and then move to the next once the first is digested, and call *that* omniscience. If the hall of Akashic Records does indeed contain every piece of knowledge and every experience that has occurred or will occur, omniscience through this medium would require that *every* crystal shard in every file cabinet into your Ajna Chakra at once. The issue with doing this, if it were even possible, would be that infinite knowledge cannot be experienced or contained by a finite form. It is therefore necessary, in order to attain omniscience, to first enter an omnipresent and omnipotent state.

To comprehend God, you must first become God.

Chapter Eleven
A Light Shining in the Darkness

"In him was life; and the life was the light of men. And the light shineth in darkness: and the darkness comprehended it not." St. John 1:4-5

The journey beyond Sat Nam, beyond the endless sea of liquid light from which all form is made manifest is no longer a journey the higher or more expanded states of being, but instead is a journey taken inwards, a folding in of the self into the self.

Passing through endless states of being and realms of existence, into the very heart of the Eternal, coming upon the realization of your own godhood – your own omnipotence, omnipresence, and omniscience – provides a sense of unity and one-ness to everything, yet at the same time leaves the individual feeling quite alienated within the human race, and yet it goes even deeper than a peerless psychological state, but becomes also a de-identification with the physical realm altogether.

Those modern thinkers who have attempted to merge mathematics and particle theory with metaphysics often refer to the limitless spiritual states described in the present work as "hyperspace," consisting of twelve dimensions which can be observed or experienced simultaneously. In fact, it is nearly impossible to experience a higher dimensional state without concomitantly experiencing all of those states preceding it. If you are only able to observe a regular object in two dimensions, viewing the length and the width of the object, experiencing some sort of visual transfiguration which would allow you to observe the third dimension of depth. The previous two dimensions are not obliterated, but simply added upon to more fully complete your observation of the object.

The revelation of that visual transfiguration would offer endless insights and realizations to the individual, so much so that an inevitable return to only two dimensions would be terrifying, a prisoner freed for only a day before being cuffed and encaged once more.

Such is the self-inflicted psychic torture of the spiritual Traveler. Over years of discipline, the initiate will learn to silence his or her body long enough to exit it, and to experience reality from an astral vantage, adding upon his or her extant knowledge of existence in the physical dimension, and will continue to add dimension upon dimension, plane upon plane, realizing along the way that this world as we view it is not illusion, it is not a dream – it is just a very limited view of the whole image.

From those planes and states and dimensions of understanding, the Traveler eventually must re-collapse his vision, reduce his awareness back to three dimensions. The residual effects, the glimmer that objects seem to take on in the minutes after returning from Soul Travel fades quickly.

In the same manner than any object approaching infinite speed encounters infinite resistance, likewise the expansion into infinite dimensionality results in an assured infinite collapse back into the finite state.

Before the Seeker even begins to seek in earnest after spiritual liberation, or before such liberation is even a feasible possibility, he or she will almost always first pass through a critical existential crisis in which the aspirant must face the question of the goodness of his or her own very existence and the place that they have not only in this world, but in all of creation. It is in this psychological dungeon that the Seeker abandons all hope of salvation, of liberation, and often even hope or care of the continuation of existence.

In his work, The Dark Night of the Soul, Saint John of the Cross considers that, as a natural part of a person's spiritual evolution, they will need to confront and triumph over any doubts that they might hold of the gospel, as well as to overcome their personal shortcomings and impurities. Such a confrontation can only be experienced through a process of intense de-identification with previous methods of spiritual fulfillment, or with spirituality as a whole.

When encountered in the realm of mysticism, however, the interesting part of the spiritual existential crisis is that seemingly in the moment of the full abandonment of any remnant of hope, the Vision appears, the heavens open, and the light and sound of the Eternal rain upon the Seeker. Addicts will often cite the "moment of clarity" that brings them out of their active addiction immediately following "hitting rock bottom."

Thus, the real process of Ascent cannot even begin until ego and ulterior motives have been leveled, and the goal is not to prove that you were able to touch the sun, but the goal is once again to simply touch the sun, for the experience itself.

The grace and surrender of the self into the Eternal currents of the spiritual that mark the whole matter of Ascent and even convergence detract from the reality that liberation itself is surrounded on all sides by despair. Ascent is hard-won, battling not only the forces of spiritual entropy which threaten at every moment to devour the Seeker, but also an ever-pressing ocean of conflict churning within the Traveler.

The battle becomes eclipsed by sudden illumination in moments, and these moments are called enlightenment and Samadhi.

When that glorious moment ebbs, on the other side of the threshold awaits a demon far worse than the one preceding it, and His name is Isolation.

A Voice in the Wilderness

Although so much has been written and postulated concerning the Dark Night of the Soul, very little is ever said about the more dreadful crisis that must be confronted *after* enlightenment has been achieved.

The realization of a greater purpose in existence is also juxtaposed by the gained understanding that everything in the lower worlds of duality is transient, and that Soul, ascended into the Heart of the Eternal, in the sea of its own power and glory, is unaffected by the circumstances and ordeals put upon the individual in physical existence. Viewing all of creation through Eternal eyes, all objects melting into a sea of light, all identities flowing out from one True Identity, the Traveler can no longer distinguish separation. He can see no difference between an enemy and his own brother, torture and truce, agony and pleasure. Living and not living.

It is said that everything is suffering, but this is a reality that can never be recognized until the seeker is dissolved into the Everlasting, and returns again to this world of suffering. This world is not suffering because of an inherent miserable quality of it, but because of the ephemeral beauty of the whole thing. Immediately after the Traveler has gained the supreme knowledge of all things, from the absence of a beginning to the absence of an end, appreciation for the luscious minutiae of life reaches an inexorable frenzy, and then quickly dwindles, a sea of bland mundanity seeming to swallow the fleeting moment of pleasure.

Most spiritual disciplines, especially those which rely heavily on mysticism, advocate cultivation of the renunciate state. By either avoiding or outright rejecting the pleasures of the flesh, the initiate hopes to sidestep the trappings of attachment, materialism, and addiction.

The renunciate model, however, seems only effective as a tool for the consecration of lust, allowing it to be hyper-generated and stored for a conclusive explosion; or as a natural retreat from an obviously decaying world once the Traveler has become aware of the evanescence not of the spiritual state, but of the physical. It would also seem that the renunciation of the flesh is taken on by achieved mystics for the latter reason, leaving the former to the adherents of kaula-tantra and the Left Hand Path.

Isolation cannot cure the malady facing the Traveler, however, and once his dire predicament is realized, his mind may move towards considerations of forcing the translation of the spiritual bodies from the physical corpse. The idea of escape from exaltation through drugs, sex, crime, and deviancy is tempting, but far from effective. He has reached a point, a degree of illumination, that cannot be negotiated or subjugated. He has leapt from a cliff over which he cannot return to the former side.

Miracles continue.

At the depth of despair, the Master has become prepared, and the student appears. Continuing the processes of Ascent and Convergence, for his own sake, seems futile, or foolish at best. When another comes across his path, however, with a fertile mind and an incessant drive, the Traveler forgets himself to instead invest in this other.

The skills and abilities developed in your own Ascent prove invaluable to those just stepping on the path, and thus the guru or the messiah is born.

The Traveler greets his new fate of mentorship with excitement, for not only does he elate with the successes of his disciples, but he literally shares in them, reaping a degree of the ecstasy and the spiritual surge of those whom he has sired through instruction and initiation.

Fitting into Infinity

The satisfaction experienced in aiding others in their Ascent, teaching them their first meditation and guiding them in their continued development is immense, but also fades quickly as you yourself continue to spiritually mature.

The state of the Messiah or the Bodhisattva in which the self is sacrificed for the enlightenment of all being with the ability of self-realization is a lesser state of spiritual Mastery. Ascent in its highest forms both relies on as well as generates nonattachment at a very core level. Indeed, it is this same transcendent nonattachment which is the root cause of the Master's malady, for he truly lives in the world yet is no longer of the world, an alien in his own home.

The need to help others, to teach others, to assist in the enlightenment of any other embodiment is not only a symptom of lingering attachment to the human form and a projection of some sort of inherent flaw in the human state, but it also seems to exacerbate the psychological and emotional atrophy, as more attachment piles on to a being who is, by his very new nature, soaring away from the world of flesh and into realms of Eternal experience.

The whole process of mentorship is a masturbatory one, wherein the Traveler seeks out others who will not only vindicate and validate his experiences but will also relate to his new sense of self. When he finds that those beings do not naturally exist, as Godhood is indeed a lonely place, he then seeks to take the clay and meat bodies surrounding him and raise them to his level, so that he will have someone that he can talk to, so that he won't feel quite so alone.

For a short while, he is sated.

The salvation of the self is not hopeless, however, and the outlines of a definite plan, of an orchestrated series of mental states and reactive behaviors can be made out. The initial despair that is felt immediately after one's enlightenment is no longer present when the joys of mentorship have passed and when it is time to drop that mantle to the floor, or at the very least such feelings have dimmed enough to allow the Traveler to operate in his body without utter contempt for the vehicle.

The Traveler emerges from his inner slumber as the embodiment of Kaulachara, an Ascendant being who can no longer identify with concepts of morality. He has dissolved his consciousness into the Eternal, and has returned with the recognition of only one remaining duality: attached and nonattached. All siddhis flow through him, yet the desire to exercise power over these lower worlds has left him; he has realized the insignificance of this world, and walks through it as a ghost, as a spectator rather than one of the players. This detached sense, which formerly led him into emotional bleakness, begins to resonate with him, begins to free him.

In his astounding work, The Yoga of Power, Julius Evola posits that, "The essence of pashaniroda, the release from bondage, is the achievement of an inner state in which the virya feels that there is nothing he is not able to do." There is a twofold statement here: the Kaula, or virya in this work, has attained the Nietzschean ideal of non-morality as well as nonattachment, therefore releasing him from the bonds of any moral restrictions, as stated above. This correlates with the second point, which is that the Kaula feels, due to the raw spiritual power that he has accumulated, that he is indeed capable of executing any feat.

His days of knighthood have passed, as has his struggle for power and control. He is left simply existing. He resigns from all concern for Dharma, for the chase after destiny's call, and dwells in simple existential bliss.

Assumption of Manforms

Despite whatever spiritual or psychological state he has risen to or sunk beneath, blending into to the human state, reintegrating into the humdrum of daily life is imperative for the Ascended Traveler. He must do this not only for the sake of those with whom he interacts, but also for his own sake, to hold onto his own sanity, to anchor himself in this world lest he drift from it forever.

An overwhelming part of the Traveler wants nothing more than to retreat from society, to live in an ashram or monastery, to do nothing but sit in meditation in every waking moment, dissolving himself into his true home and his true identity.

While this may be feasible at first, it is hardly sustainable. Those who exist as monks and hermits are *seeking* the very spiritual state that the Traveler has *attained*. The few Ascended who remain in such spiritual communities do so for the sake of the others, still attached to the idea of aiding them in Ascent, still sacrificing his own self for the ideals of the Bodhisattva.

The Traveler's newfound existential approach to his life makes the task of actually living seem less dire. Very few can live on the fringes, however, in de Sade's paradise, sampling every sin as he desires and rejecting the dross of existence. Knowing no boundaries, he is likely to go too far too often. Living by social norms seems a way to temper whatever zeal he has left for life.

The Traveler becomes, then, a realized god, capable of exacting the miraculous and experiencing the unknowable, dressed in the skin of a man, covered in jeans and button-down shirts, remembering to smile and to give hearty salutations. He is playing a role, although it is not unique to the Ascended; it is the same façade practiced by all human beings, although the Traveler is painfully aware that he is wearing the mask.

Reintegration into humanity does not necessarily take the form of complete submission to society's whims and expectations, however, but is instead a simple process of relearning how to be human. In moments of pure objectivity, embodying the inner witness, the Traveler is often alarmed and sometimes amused at how foreign the simple tasks of eating food, sleeping, making love, bathing, or even relaxing seem to him. He could become a vagabond - and some do - but he soon learns the value of having the space and the time for silence, for solitude, for entering the spiritual domains beyond as he will.

Summoning convergence, the Master will make his own little world, the microcosm of his home, his workplace, his everyday life reflective of the inner sanctity and serenity that he knows when he leaves his body. The game of manifestation will amuse him as he has his needs fulfilled quite spontaneously, and sometimes this alone is enough to keep him interested in existence.

Whatever mechanisms he constructs to assist him in simply living life, as such has indeed become an undertaking, he soon finds that he can shake another person's hand, he can engage in conversation, he can even look into their eyes, and no one would know what he is capable of. No one would suspect that they are speaking with God.

All of this is a process of becoming once again comfortable with being human, a state from which he feels entirely distant.

Solidifying the Separation

I had learned how to Travel, I had learned how to embody the Master, and had even learned how to enjoy the raw pleasure of being human once again. Success did not exist in any of these aspects of my Ascent, but instead was found in finding the balance between them. There seemed to be a great disparity between who I was internally and who I appeared to be. In one moment I was soaring beyond the known realms of spiritual existence, melting into the Eternal, recognizing that all of creation pulsated from my own vibrations and was malleable to my will; and then I remembered that I needed to take out the trash or dress appropriately for a meeting. I fantasized about the day when I would retreat to some centuries-old abandoned stone fortress in the east, seated upon a rubble of bricks, the walls around me and the earth beneath me glowing with the same power that I felt. Birds would bring me olives to eat and rain water dripped from the ceiling into my mouth.

The fantasy always ended with the realization that after three or so days of such living, the agony of the body of flesh would become unbearable, and so either the Godstate would have to diminish or the manform would have to dissolve.

Even Jesus could only bear three years of being the Messiah before he walked into his own death snare.

This disparity was a cause of a great deal of struggle for me. I could put on the mask of the man and shake the hands, smile at the faces, put in my time, and go home, but the lie was grinding on me.

How can I be God, and be a man? The two seemed contradictory in nature.

Internal compartmentalization is the key.

Many like to make a distinction between that which is secret and that which is sacred. I see no difference. That which is truly sacred cannot be shouted from the rooftops or cast before swine. And it even seemed that hiding it under a bushel basket only lit the thing on fire, revealing an even greater threat to those who looked on.

Most go their entire lives trying to piece together the fractured parts of their consciousness, looking for that lost inner child, the feminine or masculine part of themselves, or even the soul mate that is "out there... somewhere." The key to my salvation, however, was in creating a fracture, a fracture so deep that the Godself and the manform would never meet accidentally on the street.

Vows of silence turned to vows of secrecy. Tattoos were covered with Perry Ellis, waves of hair were cropped, and a shoulder-shrug replaced a disappointed shake of the head. Life had to be lived to the fullest, enjoyed to the maximum. And then, when alone, when the megalodon could harm no one, the cage would be opened.

In the morning, when the house is still asleep, a gentle, "Ahhh" breathed from my lips, and a tide of power flooded the earth after it. All that I desired came rushing to me as the tide returned. Sitting in the driver's seat of my car with the radio off and the heater wafting a slow stream of warm air towards me, my exhalations would lead me from my body into those other worlds. When I would return, a sharp breath in would collect my spiritual remnants into my chest, disbursing from there through my bloodstream until I was back in full. And then the meetings could be attended, the hands could once again be shaken, and I could invest myself fully in the moment.

This sort of life, the life of the secret Master, is like the life of a functioning drug addict. No one knows, and it makes it all the more naughty that no one knows. With the flutter of the eyelids, reality can be rearranged, yet it is a game that you play alone, with all of the world.

And somewhere in the space between the mundane and the Eternal, the Master discovers yet another degree of glory, an even more solid manifestation of power.

Chapter Twelve
The Inevitable Fall

That particular day was not unusual. It didn't stand out from any other, in any mundane way. Summer was already rushing into the desert in April, as it did each year. I always hoped that the sun would lag a little in its chase into that dreaded long season, and I was always disappointed. Autumn has always been my favorite season. The reddening leaves, the yellow grass, and the bite returning to the early morning air are wonderful, but what has always drawn me is the smell. Perhaps it is the simple fact that people begin firing up their wood-burning stoves and furnaces around October, or burning the fallen leaves piled up with garden rakes, but there always seemed to be something magical about the smoky smell accompanying the crispening air. It smelled like memories, and like mystery.

The smell of new life, rather than the comforting smell of autumnal decay, steamed all around me, blossoms already bringing fruit, the green juices of fresh cut grass somehow atomizing on the hot blades of mowers pushed by sweating workers, and the new tar on the roads wafting a petroleum stink and gaseous mirages into the heat of the midday.

My car stereo was ablaze with double-bass drums and screaming guitars, and even the louder screaming vocal, lyrics of murder and misanthropy. My elbow rested on the open window, the knuckles of my other hand riding at twelve-o-clock on the steering wheel.

I was headed home from the gym. The day's workout was not particularly intense, nor was it frustrating like it sometimes was when I didn't have the ambition to put up more weight than usual, to run longer than I had the previous day, or to maneuver into that impossible asana.

I wish that I could point to some sort of stimulus, something that set off the flash, because then I could reproduce it at will. Running through the event over and over, I can think of nothing, no visual cue, no certain scent or sound. I even listened to that same screaming song a thousand times, hoping that some subliminal message had triggered the influx. I have come up with nothing, no earthly reason that I had experienced what I had experienced in that exact moment.

While singing along to the lyrics of the song, relaxed in my bucket seat, moving down the road at an even fifty miles per hour, my vision went out. It didn't go black, it didn't narrow from the periphery as I had experienced a few times before when losing consciousness. My vision went white. White isn't even the right color. My whole field of vision was flooded with more light than what my eyes were capable of beholding. In that same instant, a bell the size of Manhattan chimed all around me, deafening, and the drone of that bell continued for a half of an hour from that single invisible strike. My chest seized, not in pain, but in the most terrifying peace and horrendous love that I had ever felt.

My foot moved to the brake pedal, more calmly than perhaps it should have, as I had no way to be sure of what was in front of me as all of my senses were too overwhelmed to deal with this world any longer. I let the car drift to the right until the tires nudged the curb, telling me that I was out of the way of traffic. Somewhere inside of me a voice tried to squeal at me to panic, to slam on the brakes and to exit my car flailing. The certain yet illogical knowledge that I would come to no harm drowned out that small voice until it could no longer be heard at all.

I put the manual transmission into neutral, jiggling the shifter until I could feel that it was floating between the gears, and I released the clutch and depressed the parking brake.

My eyes were open, but I could not see this world at all. The light that had blinded me began to move like smoke, only it flowed down to the earth rather than up to the sky. As rings of light moved over me, my blinded eyes filled with tears and my body shook, the physical self not competent in coping with such a crushing sense of wellness, of perfection, of ultimate completeness in all things. After almost thirty minutes the light ascended, lifting off from me, and returned to whatever celestial source had commanded it. My vision returned, and the droning of the bell weakened, and I could feel my heart racing as if I had mainlined amphetamines, which I can only assure you that I did not.

I noticed that the music was still playing from my car stereo, although I had forgotten about it through the din of the violent spiritual embrace. I clicked off the stereo, unbuckled my safety belt, curled my body into itself, and sobbed.

I had experienced moments of absolute peace, moments of profound serenity, even days of oneness with all, but no intensity of spiritual surge and experience had ever shaken me like that. It was a baptism, not of water nor of fire, but of light.

Enlightenment comes in various degrees. It has come to me as an extra-intellectual understanding of things, or as a surety beyond words of an idea. On that day, however, enlightenment took the form of Baraq-El; the Lightening of God.

From an objective view, it would appear that the Seeker will devote himself to the task of enlightenment, which will eventually be delivered to him in a glorious flash of super comprehension, after which he will then be "Enlightened."

Again, Ascent is hard-won, battling not only the forces of spiritual entropy which threaten at every moment to devour the Seeker, but also an ever-pressing ocean of conflict churning within the Traveler. The battle becomes eclipsed by sudden illumination in moments, and these moments are called enlightenment and Samadhi.

The life of the Traveler must become one of stillness, an ongoing meditation, for it is in that silent space that his Lover enters, and they unite, and the flash of illumination is had. While one cannot force enlightenment, cannot summon it like a demon from the depths, the thing can certainly be tempted to come, to deliver its fruits, when the vessel is prepared and is attractive to the power.

Had such a flash of Eternal perfection fallen on me daily as it did that day in my car, that which I call Soul would begin to seek out greater moments of enlightenment, higher and more profound degrees of revelation. Repetition breeds familiarity; familiarity breeds contempt; contempt breeds initiative to reach beyond the repetitive and contemptuous circumstance.

I have gone on at length in the preceding chapters on the spiritual, psychological, and emotional morass into which the Traveler will inevitably fall once he has attained even a degree of enlightenment, and has broken free of duality by penetrating through the veils of the other worlds. Not only the frail mind and the tenuous heart respond to such a violation of the laws of Maya by shattering, but the Maya world around the Traveler begins to break as well.

This is not to say that Maya, illusion, begins to break, because that fissure has already widened into a ravine. Instead, the scattered pieces of the lower worlds begin to move, not in conspiracy to annihilate the Traveler, although this will undoubtedly seem to be the case. Instead, it is as if the whole of existence begins to cooperate, for the first time, in the ultimate perfection of the individual.

Not only does each person possess traits, addictions, or flaws that hold him back from his highest potential, but nearly everyone can smile and list them without pause. We often hold to these habits as if they were tethers or kite strings, without which we would float off into the ether of eternity. The Traveler may feel that his vices are what anchors him to the human state. Through the process of Ascent, however, as well as automatic Convergence, these vices are eliminated, the tether is severed, and he has no choice but to embrace that which he can become.

This is a terrifying thing to face, especially in the light of all that he has done to stave off the inner darkness with which he was assaulted as he returned from the other worlds to his body. Left with a choice, he would linger in between godhood and mortality, that comfortable nether-realm of masks and secrets. The secrets will not lift, and the public mask will remain, but again, he has no choice. His Ascent has already brought him this far, and the momentum will not cease.

All of those things, which hold the Traveler back, which ground him in his human state, are removed, quite unceremoniously. He has been given the chance to reform his life, to put away all that binds him, and having neglected the call, all vice is ripped from him, with all of the powers of these lower worlds moving against him, for his benefit.

This will seem as a second Dark Night of the Soul, as if those very forces which have become his constant companion have abandoned him, as he finds himself imprisoned, destitute, divorced, disfellowshipped, and disowned. All of this is a simple method of removing obstacles, either internal or environmental. Once the Traveler's life is clear of such impediments, those same powers rush down, freeing him from bars and restoring all that was taken from him. He will suffer the mundane consequences of his vices only long enough to retreat from them.

These alterations in the way that the Traveler lives his life are not in accordance with some universal code of ethics, but are instead dictated by his own personal morals. He has gone beyond duality, beyond right and wrong, good and evil, even beyond compassion and hatred. What remains that can even be called "morals" are a set of modes of behavior, which he has found most suitable to his emotional and intellectual being. If anything causes negative attachment, that thing can be considered "bad." The violation of those personal morals sets the whole of the universe at odds with the Traveler until balance has been restored.

Once such a purging has been completed, the Traveler will then find that he has entered an entirely new spiritual and psychological space wherein that which can be called Karma, which is really the effect of Supersoul intervening to eliminate attachment, no longer waits lifetimes, years, or even days to bring the subject back into balance, but instead exacts its corrective measures instantaneously.

Just as enlightenment comes in a sudden wave and then departs, so does this state of self-purification and continual perfection. The first few stages of this cleansing consist of removing those things that we know without hesitation to be amiss. Subsequent purifying events will take place to clear away rubble of which we were never even aware. Our attachments will fall like enemies before a warlord, and we will rise with a smile to continue the game again.

What is most interesting is that during these periods of purification, all spiritual progress will seem to have halted. Even for months it will seem as though something as simple as meditation is blocked, and the blockage occurs simultaneous with the minor details of life falling apart. Relationships will crumble, finances will deteriorate, automobiles will go from pristine to dilapidated within hours.

Just as with the greater purifications of imprisonment and destruction, all things are restored in the very moment that all hope is eclipsed, and the previous bounty is added to. The relationships that are severed are replaced with even greater ones, or are returned with an increased vigor; money will again flow, in even greater amounts and with greater ease than before; the repairs for the automobile will go from debilitating to feasible, or a new vehicle will be delivered. All waters are made aright.

There seems to be an exact cycle, tailored to each Traveler. Once you are able to identify the specific signs of your own purification period, a car breaking down or a monetary loss will cause you to smile, because it is clear that once the cycle has run its course, your life and your entire being will be elevated.

It is important during these periods, however, to notice the exact situations that are being shaken, as these are your attachments. Nothing has to be done, for the power to resolve all difficulties lies in non-action. All that is necessary is to realize that you have allowed the balance between the manform and the Godself to shift to the physical.

Chapter Thirteen
The Anti-Transmigratory Experience

All of this discussion on the methods and the effects of illumination has been quite mundane, dealing with the personal experience of Ascent and Convergence. What of the greater aspects of it all?

Have no doubt that, having come this far, you have become God made flesh. It is not your lot to simply act like another of the herd and to wither away in a quiet existence. It is your place to be a Master among men. But you cannot simply stand on the walls of the city and preach hellfire, or declare that you are Ipsissimus incarnate. That kind of behavior will get you crucified.

All lower dharmas have been obliterated by your journey into the heart of the Eternal, yet there is a Destiny which still remains, which still calls, only more faintly than before. It is no longer necessary for the heavens to shout their decree to your ears, for your will and the will of the Eternal have merged.

You are God, but you are an infant god. You must look at your fingers and your toes, wiggling every divine appendage that you discover, deciphering how this new Limitless body operates.

Your breath moving in and out is the blood flow of the life of the world. You are the heart, and your power is the beating of it on the walls of the universe's chest.

There is nothing that you cannot do. The most difficult task, now, is to choose something to do. All attachment, all desire has fled from you. All Siddhis are yours, yet all thirst for power has drained into the pool of eternity.

Although you have come farther than most mortals ever will, there is still farther yet to go. There are orders of beings beyond the Masters, there are Temples of Knowledge beneath the sea of liquid light, and in order to reach into these most secret places, the whole of your being must be prepared.

You can travel in Soul through the planes of existence, and can dissolve yourself into omnipresence. The reverse is also true. From omnipresence, you can be gathered into one spot on the lower planes, and can manifest there. If your focal point is your body, which it most often will be, you will momentarily shine like a thousand suns before the walls are erected to save your sanity and to protect your body from the lashings of infinitude. If your focus is brought to a place outside of your body, however, for an equally minute moment, you will materialize in that place, and then your specter will vanish back into the ether. This is a power that I have only toyed with, producing interesting results for those who have witnessed and have later reported that for a moment they swore that they saw me. This is a siddhi that I have yet to master, however, in order to maintain such a disembodied critical mass for more than a moment.

Upon the death of your body, you may go to Lord Yama in the hall of sorrows, and you may steal his scepter and his crown and continue on past the need for judgment, past the requirements of energetic recycling, and you may plunge into the ocean of the Eternal. Or, you may enter into omnipresence and focus your rematerialization into the body of a woman, being born again into this lowest plane, to play this play once more.

You are the Master of Destiny, and that is your only destiny.

Works Cited

Foreword

1. Crowley, Aleister. Magick in Theory and Practice. Master Therion. 1929.

Chapter One

1. Brady, Ian. The Gates of Janus. Ferrel House, 2001.
2. This quote is taken from my conversations with a spiritual Master.

Chapter Three

1. Evola, Julius. The Yoga of Power: Tantra, Shakti, and the Secret Way. Inner Traditions International. 1992.

Chapter Four

1. The Door to December was a book published in 1985 by Signet Publications, and authored by Dean Koontz. The Door to December discusses, in a fictional format, the use of such mental trickeries in order to unlock the latent psychic abilities of the subjects of these experiments.

Part III

Ipsissimus

1. The New Testament, books of Matthew, Mark, Luke, and John.
2. Prophet, Elizabeth Claire. <u>Saint Germain on Alchemy</u>. Summit University Press. 1988.

Chapter Nine

1. Saint John of the Cross. <u>The Dark Night of the Soul</u>.

www.ingramcontent.com/pod-product-compliance
Lightning Source LLC
Chambersburg PA
CBHW031932090426
42811CB00002B/157